ANNOTATED CHECKLIST OF THE BIRDS OF CUBA

Number 2
2018-2019

Nils Navarro Pacheco

www.EdicionesNuevosMundos.com

Senior Editor: Nils Navarro Pacheco

Editors: Soledad Pagliuca, Kathleen Hennessey and Sharyn Thompson

Covers Design: Scott Shiller

Cover: Cuban Pygmy Owl (*Glaucidium siju*), Peralta, Zapata Swamp, Matanzas, Cuba. Photo Nils Navarro Pacheco, 2017

Back cover Illustrations: Nils Navarro, © Endemic Birds of Cuba. A Comprehensive Field Guide, 2015

Published by Ediciones Nuevos Mundos
www.EdicionesNuevosMundos.com
sole@edicionesnuevosmundos.com

Annotated Checklist of the Birds of Cuba
©Nils Navarro Pacheco, 2018
©Ediciones Nuevos Mundos, 2018

ISBN: 9781790608690

*To the memory of Jim Wiley, a great friend, extraordinary person and scientist, a guiding light of Caribbean ornithology.
He crossed many troubled waters in pursuit of expanding our knowledge of Cuban birds.*

About the Author

Nils Navarro Pacheco was born in Holguín, Cuba. He is a freelance author and an internationally acclaimed wildlife artist and scientific illustrator. A graduate of the Academy of Fine Arts with a major in painting, he served as curator of the herpetological collection of the Holguín Museum of Natural History, where he described several new species of lizards and frogs for Cuba.

Nils has been travelling throughout the Caribbean Islands and Central America working on different projects related to the conservation of biodiversity, with a particular focus on amphibians and birds. He is the author of the book *Endemic Birds of Cuba, A Comprehensive Field Guide*, which, enriched by his own illustrations, creates a personalized field guide structure that is both practical and useful, with icons as substitutes for texts. It also includes other important features based on his personal experience and understanding of the needs of field guide users. Nils continues to contribute his artwork and copyrights to BirdsCaribbean, other NGOs, and national and international institutions in an effort to help raise funds in support of bird conservation in the Caribbean region. Nils is currently an eBird reviewer for Cuba, and author of the *Annotated Checklist of the Birds of Cuba*, an annual publication that has become the official list of the birds of Cuba. Currently he is working on a new *Comprehensive Field Guide to the Birds of Cuba*.

The Annotated Checklist of the Birds of Cuba is an annual publication that grew from the need to provide updated information about changes that have affected birds registered in the Cuban archipelago. Development of new techniques in molecular studies, new interpretations of speciation and evolutionary phenomena have also emerged, considerably modifying the traditional way of viewing ornithology and resulting in rapid changes in taxonomy and systematics, often beyond what we can assimilate through the normal flow of information.

In addition, the growing demand for bird-watching tourism on the island and the implementation of monitoring programs of migratory species are contributing to an increase in the number of previously unregistered species entering the list every year. Furthermore, the influence of climate change is producing altered patterns of migratory movements in many species.

Our main objective is to provide up-to-date annual listings of Cuban birds, including reference information on each new report and general statistics about Cuban birdlife, and to serve as a reference platform for ornithological studies in the country. It is our obligation to make continuous efforts to make this publication accessible to the community of local ornithologists and to the institutions involved in the conservation and study of Cuban birds.

Nils Navarro
Senior Editor

Contents

Acknowledgements 8
Before using the checklist 9
    Listed Species 9
    Taxonomic Sequence 9
    English Name 10
    Local Name 10
    Scientific Name 10
    Subspecies 10
    Threat Status 11
    Endemic Region 11
    Abundance status 12
    Breeding Status 12
    Resident Status 12
    Introduced 13
    Distribution 13
About eBird 15
Annotated Checklist of the Birds of Cuba 16
    Order: ANSERIFORMES 16
    Order: GALLIFORMES 17
    Order: PHOENICOPTERIFORMES 17
    Order: PODICIPEDIFORMES 17
    Order: COLUMBIFORMES 17
    Order: CUCULIFORMES 18
    Order: CAPRIMULGIFORMES 18
    Order: NYCTIBIIFORMES 18
    Order: APODIFORMES 18
    Order: GRUIFORMES 18
    Order: CHARADRIIFORMES 19
    Order: PHAETHONTIFORMES 22
    Order: GAVIIFORMES 22
    Order: PROCELLARIIFORMES 22
    Order: CICONIIFORMES 22
    Order: SULIFORMES 22
    Order: PELECANIFORMES 23
    Order: CATHARTIFORMES 23
    Order: ACCIPITRIFORMES 24
    Order: STRIGIFORMES 24
    Order: TROGONIFORMES 25
    Order: CORACIIFORMES 25

- Order: PICIFORMES ... 25
- Order: FALCONIFORMES ... 25
- Order: PSITTACIFORMES ... 25
- Order: PASSERIFORMES ... 26

Hypothetical Species ... 33

Other exotics, introduced and uncertain origin species ... 33

GENERAL COMMENTS ... 36
- New additions ... 36
- Comments ... 37

Species added to the list in the previous issue of the Checklist (2017) ... 50

Cuban Birds, Numbers and Percentages ... 51

References ... 52

Notes ... 59

Acknowledgements

Each issue of this publication has been made possible thanks to the help of many friends, colleagues, institutions and NGO's.

Special thanks to Javier Torres and Bárbara Sánchez (Baby) who helped create a databank of publications about Cuban birds; their kind support in finding every paper was crucial to the preparation of this issue. To Orlando Garrido, Herbert Raffaelle, Jim Wiley†, Alejandro Llanes, Jeff Gerbratch, Lisa Sorenson, Andrea Holbrook, Gary Markowski, Natalia Rossi, Maikel Cañizares, Andy Mitchel, Carlos Peña, Rafaella Aguilera, Xotchilt Ayón, and Alina Perez for their contributions, ideas, time and support. Thanks to "The Pamela and Alexander F. Skutch Research Award for Studies in Avian Natural History" of The Association of Field Ornithologists; their support made it possible to increase the information related to Cuban avifauna, in particular with relation to Critically Endangered species.

To Birds Caribbean, Holbrook Travel, eBird Team, Ediciones Nuevos Mundos, Cuban Society of Zoology, WhiteHawk, Caribbean Conservation Trust, Optics for the Tropics, and Wildlife Conservation Society.

To Scott Shiller who kindly created wonderful designs for this issue and dedicated much of his time to working on it, my most sincere thanks!

My sincere thanks to (in alphabetical order): Alejandro Barro, Alieny Rodríguez, Angel Muela, Ansel Font, Anthony Levesque, Ariam Jiménez, Ann Sutton, Aslam Ibrahim Castellón, Bárbara Sánchez, Bárbara López, Beny Wilson, Carlos Hernández Peraza, Dennis LePage, Edelys Figueredo, Edwin Rojas, Elissa Landre, Ernesto Reyes, Feliberto Bermúdez (Felix), Frantz Delcroix (Duzont), Giraldo Alayón, Hiram González, Ianela Lau, Ivalut Ruiz, Jeremiah Trimble, Jim Wiley†, Joni Ellis, Jocelyne Pelletier, Jorge Luis Guerra, Jorge Uria, José Fernández Ordóñez, Giraldo Alayón, Greg Homel, Josep del Hoyo, Julio César Hernández (César), Kathleen Hennessey, Kenia Medina, Lourdes Mujica, Marta Curti, Martín Acosta, Marvin and Lee Cook, Michael Good, Miguel Angel Acosta (Migue), Mirza Pérez, Moth Clarck, Odey Martinez, Orestes Martínez (El Chino Zapata), Paul Baicich, Paulino López, Pedro Regalado, Reinaldo Rodríguez (Chito), Robert Norton, Rodolfo Castro (Fofito), Rogelio Quintana senior and junior, Rolando Rodríguez Atá, Sharyn E. Thompson, Soledad Pagliuca, Suray Soto, Wayne Petersen, Wayne Fidler, Yaroddy Rodríguez, Yehudi Hernández, Yeray Seminario, and Zoyla Pacheco.

To the team at Ediciones Nuevos Mundos: Sole, Kate and Sharyn, with my eternal appreciation for their exceptional job and patience.

To my wife Yerenia, my sons Diego, Alejandro and Noel, my parents, brother and little granddaughter Ashley (Susana) thanks for allowing me to steal the time I should have dedicated to the family.

To the eBird community who, with their observations, contribute every day to broaden the knowledge of the birds in Cuba and around the world.

Before using the checklist

It is very important to read the following section carefully in order to learn how to understand each category. For example, to get a better understanding of the category "Abundance Status", it must be linked with each "Distribution pattern". A species that may look Uncommon on the island could appear as Fairly Common due its distribution status: Local, Regional or Quasi-Cuban.

Listed Species

The forms (intended as species or subspecies) listed here are those for which there is a specimen; clearly distinctive sound recording; diagnostic photograph or a description that reflects familiarity with the species; fits distinctive field marks; and clearly distinguishes this species from similar species. eBird sightings were also considered when validated by the eBird reviewer team. We include reference citations and comments (in superscript numbers and letters) for the more recent or rare records, and when further important information is needed to clarify its status.

The basic terms and concept of this checklist were adapted to local conditions from Gerbracht and Levesque (unpublished).

Improved alignment and consolidation of independent taxonomic studies are goals of the newly restructured International Ornithologists´ Union (IOU). List editors and interested colleagues participated in a vigorous Round Table discussion and follow-up at the August 2018 Congress in Vancouver, British Columbia. There was broad consensus and support for a global checklist of birds to serve as the standard reference for the class Aves. Consequently, Dick Schodde and Frank Gill submitted a proposal to the IOU Executive Committee to form a Working Group on Global Avian Checklists, chaired by Les Christidis, to achieve that goal.

As we lack an international taxonomic consensus yet, this new edition has been updated with the latest taxonomic changes following the 59th AOS Supplement (Chesser *et al.*, 2018). It is important to note that this checklist will no longer publish records of new sightings, as that is not the main goal of this publication. New records can be uploaded to eBird.

This checklist also includes changes in sequences working at the subspecific level, whereas in the first issue we listed just the species level. Some species have been moved from the main list to the supplementary lists and a new table with the hypothetical records is included. To support more accurate information I decided to include a column with distributional categories for each species. The new integrated concept makes this checklist more practical, where the goal of comments is to clarify incongruencies generated by the use of different taxonomic philosophies among the world lists currently in use and other important data.

Taxonomic Sequence

The order in which taxa are sorted is based on the *eBird/Clements Checklist v2017* (http://www.birds.cornell.edu), which combines all taxa from the Clements Checklist and all additional categories from the eBird taxonomy. Sequences could vary depending on the taxonomic philosophy. Lists such as *IOC World List*; *Handbook of the Birds of the World Alive*; *British Ornithological Union List*; and *The Howard & Moore Complete Checklist of the Birds of the World, 4th Edition* follow other taxonomic criteria and sequence order.

This checklist follows the North American Classification Committee (NACC), which operates under the philosophy and procedures outlined in the Preface to the 7th edition (NACC). Although the Committee recognizes the controversy over species concepts in ornithology, it generally adheres to the principles of the Biological Species Concept. Multiple lines of evidence (e.g., multiple genetic loci, or genes plus other traits) are favored over single data sets for taxonomic changes at species and higher levels. The Committee prefers to act conservatively in its treatments of taxonomy and nomenclature; thus, proposals that suggest but do not strongly support taxonomic change, or that cause instability, may be rejected pending further data. Generally, at least two independent datasets are required for making changes at higher-level classifications.

English Name

The English common name for each species as defined by the most current version of eBird/Clements Checklist v2018 (http://www.birds.cornell.edu).

This checklist follows the NACC policy on English names, which is stated in the Forward to the 6th (1983) edition of the *Check-list of North American Birds*, and is further elaborated by AOU Committee, 2007.

Local Name

The Cuban Common Name (CCN) is the one used throughout the country to refer to any specific bird, according to Garrido and Kirkconnell, 2011. They are not always the same as the standardized names in Spanish used by SEO/BirdLife Int. (Sociedad Española de Ornitología) or similar. The CCN is useful for communication within the country. There are also other local names that are not included in this checklist. Keep in mind that some CCN could vary in pronunciation; often the local people contract words such as Carpintero Jabado, which becomes Carpintero Jabao, or Rabudita, which becomes Rabuita.

For recent inclusion of new records in the Checklist we use the SEO name, as there is no CCN yet.

Scientific Name

The scientific name for each species as defined by the most current version of the *eBird/Clements Checklist v2018* (www.birds.cornell.edu/clementschecklist/download/). All have been updated with the latest changes in the 59th AOS Supplement (Chesser *et al.*, 2018).

This checklist follows the AOS Committee on Classification and Nomenclature of North and Middle American Birds (NACC) which operates on a proposal basis. Proposals are submitted and reviewed for taxonomic changes, English name changes, acceptance of distributional records, and other items related to the charge of the Committee.

Subspecies

The last edition of the AOU Checklist to include subspecies was published in 1957 (5th edition). For reasons of expediency, the Committee reluctantly excluded treatment of subspecies in both the 6th and 7th editions.

Subspecies reflect biological diversity and play an important role in flagging the attention of evolutionary, behavioral, ecological, and conservation biologists. After careful study, an unknown number of subspecies likely will unmask cryptic biological species, or "species-in-the-making" that constitute a significant element of newly evolving biodiversity. On the other hand, an uncertain number of current subspecies apply to poorly differentiated populations and thus cannot be validated by rigorous modern techniques.

Although a complete revision of North American avian subspecies has not been done, I refer readers to Avibase and the Birds of North America Online for more up-to-date treatments of subspecies. The Birds of North America project is systematically revising subspecies accounts for North American birds.

As other primary world bird lists differ slightly in their primary goals and taxonomic philosophy I decided to follow the *eBird/Clements Checklist v2017* (www.birds.cornell.edu) which matches the treatment commonly used in the North, Middle-American and Caribbean area, adding comments to those entries that differ from other world lists in the way they integrate taxonomic points of view.

Threat Status

IUCN categories and criteria (version 3.1, see www.iucnredlist.org for more details), are listed in bold and identify the worldwide status along the species' entire distribution range. For the Cuban assessment we followed the updated criteria in González et al., 2012 which is based on the IUCN Standards and Petitions Working Group. The data in italics applies to the assessment of the Cuban population status; it has been enriched and updated by local specialists (González et al., 2012); it clarifies when the IUCN criteria differs. Uncertain status is designated by a question mark (?).

Extinct (Ex) A taxon is Extinct when there is no reasonable doubt that the last individual has died. A species is presumed Extinct when exhaustive surveys in known and/or expected habitat, at appropriate times (diurnal, seasonal, annual), throughout its historic range have failed to record an individual. Surveys should be over a time frame appropriate to the species' life history.

Critically Endangered (CR): A taxon is Critically Endangered when the best available evidence (severe population decline, very small population, very small geographic area occupied, or if the calculated probability of extinction during the next 10 years is >50%) indicates that it is facing an extremely high risk of extinction in the wild.

Endangered (EN): A taxon is Endangered when the best available evidence (large population decline, small population, small geographic area occupied, or if the calculated probability of extinction during the next 20 years is >20%) indicates that it is considered to be facing a very high risk of extinction in the wild.

Vulnerable (VU): A taxon is Vulnerable when the best available evidence (large population decline, small population, small geographic area occupied, or if the calculated probability of extinction during the next 20 years is at least 10%) indicates that it is considered to be facing a very high risk of extinction in the wild.

Near Threatened (NT): A taxon is Near Threatened when it has been evaluated against the criteria but does not qualify for Critically Endangered, Endangered or Vulnerable now, but is close to qualifying for or is likely to qualify for a threatened category in the near future.

Least Concern (LC): A taxon is Least Concern when it has been evaluated against the criteria and does not qualify for Critically Endangered, Endangered, Vulnerable or Near Threatened. Widespread and abundant species are included in this category.

Endemic Region

The endemic region is the most restrictive overarching region of endemism for each endemic species, i.e., a species that occurs in both the Greater and Lesser Antilles is considered a West Indian endemic, whereas a species that is endemic to Cuba and Hispaniola is considered a Greater Antillean endemic.

West Indies (WI): A form that is not restricted to a single region but is restricted to islands in the West Indies.

Greater Antilles (GA): A form that is restricted to islands in the Greater Antilles (Cuba, Jamaica, Puerto Rico and Hispaniola).

Western Caribbean (WC): A form that also includes islands on the Western Caribbean, i.e., San Andrés and Providencia.

Cuba (CU): A form that is restricted to the Cuban archipelago.

Cayman Islands (CI): A form that also occurs on Cayman Islands; Cuba shares some near endemic species with these islands.

Lucayan (LY): A form that also occurs on islands in the Lucayan Archipelago (Bahamas, Turks and Caicos).

Abundance status
These are relative concepts to measure a bird observation frequency; in general this checklist follows the ranges given by Herbert Raffaelle *et al.* (1998), which focuses on West Indian birds.

There is no complete study of the abundance of every Cuban bird species; consequently there are gaps in this knowledge. In some cases I have had to rely on historical records and information gathered from collections. I have also used the total number of sightings combined with the migratory sources areas, and calculated the real probability that a new sighting will occur. Specifying a range for each category only applies to Rare (R), Very Rare (VR) and Exceptionally Rare (XR).

Common (Co): A form that occurs in high frequency. Five or more individuals likely to be seen daily in the appropriate habitat and season.

Fairly Common (FC): A form that occurs in moderate frequency. 1-4 individuals likely to be seen daily in the appropriate habitat and season.

Uncommon (U): A form that occurs in low frequency. Not likely to be seen on every expedition, but can be seen at least twice per year.

Rare (R): Fewer than two records per year; expect at least one occurrence every 5 years or more than three sightings to 50 sightings in total.

Very Rare (VR): Occurs once every 6 to 10 years or those species that had up to two sightings in total and came from traditional migrant sources such as North or South America.

Exceptionally Rare (XR): A form with only one sighting that occurs exceptionally. Usually vagrant birds that do not come from traditional migratory sources areas (Middle America, Old World or non-migratory species). Also applies to the special cases of Critically Endangered species such as Zapata Rail, Ivory-billed Woodpecker or Cuban Kite with very few officially recognized sightings.

†: A form that is extinct globally.

Breeding Status
Breeding (Br): A form that reproduces within the Cuban archipelago.

Non-Breeding (-): A form that does not reproduce within the Cuban archipelago.

Resident Status
The terms follow *The Birdwatcher's Dictionary*, Peter Weaver (1981) in the *Authoritative Dictionary of Birdwatching Terminology* (www.birdcare.com), adapted to the similar terminologies currently in use in the region.

Year Round (YR): A form that is likely to occur throughout the entire year.

Partial Migrant (PM): A form in which some individuals are resident but others are involved in migration outside the island. Shows in superindex when the condition is potentially secondary, or indicates winter (W) or summer (S) condition.

Summer Resident (SR): A bird which uses a particular area for breeding only, therefore is absent outside the breeding season. In Cuba birds arrive from South America (usually February–September, early migrants, late January). Shows in superindex when the condition is potentially secondary. Also known as "Summer Visitor".

Winter Resident (WR): A bird that visits a particular area only for the winter and does not breed there. As the Cuban archipelago has a tropical climate year-round, it hosts many WR from North America (mainly September to May but early migrants could arrive in July). Shows in superindex when the condition is potentially secondary.

Transient (T): Movement through an area involving individuals who neither breed nor spend the winter here, merely passing through on migration. As the Cuban archipelago lies on a major flyway, very large numbers of Transients travel through each spring and autumn (mainly September – October and April – May).

Vagrant (V): A bird that wanders to a particular area if its orientation is at fault or adverse winds drive it off course, but under normal circumstances would not be found in Cuba. Vagrants are also called "accidentals" or "casuals".

Note: Many species have different timings of migration and the actual month ranges for these seasonality values will be different among species.

Introduced
This checklist follows the British Ornithologist Union set of definitions for introduced species. (www.bou.org.uk/british-list/species-categories/).

Category C:
A form whose presence results from human introduction and is now derived in self-sustaining populations.

(C1): *Naturalized introduced populations* – species that occur only as a result of introduction.

(C2): *Naturalized established species* – species with established populations resulting from introduction by humans, but which also occur in an apparently natural state.

(C3): *Naturalized re-established species* – species with populations successfully re-established by humans in areas of former occurrence.

(C4): *Naturalized feral species* – domesticated species with populations established in the wild.

(C5): *Vagrant naturalized species* – species from established naturalized populations abroad.

(C6): *Former naturalized species* – species formerly placed in C1 whose naturalized populations are either no longer self-sustaining or are considered extinct.

Category E:
Species recorded as introductions, human-assisted transportees or escapees from captivity, and whose breeding populations (if any) are thought not to be self-sustaining.

Distribution
Pan-Cuban (PC): widespread along the archipelago in the appropriate habitat and season.

Quasi-Cuban (QC): with a wide distribution range but absent in part of the country in the appropriate habitat and season.

Regional distribution (Rg): Species are restricted only to a particular region: Eastern, Central or Western Cuba, e.g., Yellow-headed Warbler lives only in western Cuba.

Local (L): Species with very limited distribution mainly restricted to one or few sites, e.g., Zapata Wren in Zapata Swamp.

Punctual (P): Species recorded in very few sites, usually sightings of vagrant birds.

About eBird

eBird is an online database of bird observations that provides scientists, researchers and amateur naturalists with real-time data about bird distribution and abundance. Originally restricted to sightings from the Western Hemisphere, by 2010 it covered the whole world. eBird has been described as an ambitious example of enlisting amateurs to gather data on biodiversity for use in science that has become an incredibly useful tool.

eBird is an example of crowdsourcing, and has been hailed as an example of democratizing science, treating citizens as scientists, allowing the public to access and use their own data and the collective data generated by others.

eBird's goal is to maximize the utility and accessibility of the vast numbers of bird observations made each year by recreational and professional bird watchers. The observations of each participant join those of others in an international network. Due to the variability in the observations the volunteers make, eBird filters observations through collected historical data to improve accuracy. The data are then available via internet queries in a variety of formats.

Some tips to get better results uploading your list to eBird:

- Be sure that the sightings are well identified and placed in the right location. Include local names if possible.
- Close the list when you finish one site and continue to another location.
- When you use a mobile phone be sure to make the right selection of the species on the list; sometimes fingers unintentionally flag the next or previous species on the list.
- In the case of Rare species please add comments that explain the field marks used in the ID. The eBird reviewers will appreciate it very much, and a clear ID will help in the validation process of the sighting.
- When possible, add photos, videos, and recordings, especially with species marked as Rare for the area.
- New records of species for Cuba need to be supported by graphic information such as photos, videos or any kind of proof that supports the validation of the sighting.

This checklist is eBird friendly; it integrates the eBird names and forms making it easier for the eBird user to upload the data.

Annotated Checklist of the Birds of Cuba

	English Name/ Cuban Common Name (CCN)/ *Latin Name*	Threat status	End. Reg.	Abun. status	Breed status	Resid. status	Int.	Dist.
	Order: ANSERIFORMES Family: Anatidae							
1.	☐ **White-faced Whistling-Duck**/Yaguasa Cariblanca/ *Dendrocygna viduata*	LC	-	R	-	V	-	P
2.	☐ **Black-bellied Whistling-Duck (fulgens)**/Yaguasa Barriguiprieta/ *Dendrocygna autumnalis fulgens*[1]	LC	-	R	?	YR	-	P
3.	☐ **West Indian Whistling-Duck**/Yaguasa Cubana/*Dendrocygna arborea*	VU	WI	FC	Br	YR	-	PC
4.	☐ **Fulvous Whistling-Duck**/Yaguasín/*Dendrocygna bicolor*	LC	-	FC	Br	PM[W2]	-	PC
5.	☐ **Snow Goose**/Guanana Prieta/*Anser caerulescens caerulescens*	LC	-	R	-	V	-	P
6.	☐ **Greater White-fronted Goose (Western)**/Guanana/*Anser albifrons gambelli*	LC	-	R	-	V	-	P
7.	☐ **Canada Goose (canadensis Group)**/Ganso de Canadá/*Branta canadensis canadensis*	LC	-	VR	-	V	-	P
8.	☐ **Tundra Swan (Whistling)**/Cisne de la Tundra/*Cygnus columbianus columbianus*	LC	-	VR	-	V	-	P
9.	☐ **Muscovy Duck (Established Feral)**/Pato Doméstico/*Cairina moschata*	LC	-	U	Br	YR	C4	PC
10.	☐ **Wood Duck** Pato Huyuyo/*Aix sponsa*	LC	-	FC	Br	PM	-	PC
11.	☐ **Blue-winged Teal**/Pato de la Florida/*Spatula discors*	LC	-	Co	?	WR[PM3]	-	PC
12.	☐ **Cinnamon Teal**/Pato Canelo/*Spatula cyanoptera septentrionalis*	LC	-	U	-	WR	-	P
13.	☐ **Northern Shoveler**/Pato Cuchareta/*Spatula clypeata*	LC	-	FC	-	WR-T	-	PC
14.	☐ **Gadwall (Common)**/Pato Gris/*Mareca strepera strepera*	LC	-	R	-	WR	-	P
15.	☐ **Eurasian Wigeon**/Pato Eurasiático/*Mareca penelope*	LC	-	VR	-	V	-	P
16.	☐ **American Wigeon**/Pato Lavanco/*Mareca americana*	LC	-	FC	-	WR-T	-	PC
17.	☐ **Mallard (Northern)**/Pato Inglés/*Anas platyrhynchos platyrhynchos*	LC	-	R	-	WR-T	-	P
18.	☐ **American Black Duck**/Pato Negro Americano/*Anas rubripes*	LC	-	VR	-	V	-	P
19.	☐ **White-cheeked Pintail (White-cheeked)**/Pato de Bahamas/*Anas bahamensis bahamensis*	LC	-	FC	Br	YR	-	PC
20.	☐ **Northern Pintail**/Pato Pescuecilargo/*Anas acuta*	LC	-	FC	-	WR-T	-	PC
21.	☐ **Green-winged Teal (American)**/Pato Serrano/*Anas crecca carolinensis*	LC	-	FC	-	WR-T	-	PC
22.	☐ **Canvasback**/Pato Lomiblanco/*Aythya valisineria*	LC	-	R	-	WR	-	P
23.	☐ **Redhead**/ Pato Cabecirrojo/ *Aythya americana*	LC	-	VR	-	V	-	P
24.	☐ **Ring-necked Duck**/Pato Cabezón/*Aythya collaris*	LC	-	Co	-	WR-T	-	PC
25.	☐ **Lesser Scaup**/Pato Morisco/*Aythya affinis*	LC	-	Co	-	WR-T	-	PC
26.	☐ **Surf Scoter**/Negrón Careto (SEO)/*Melanitta perspicillata*	LC	-	VR	-	V	-	P
27.	☐ **White-winged Scoter (North American)**/Negrón Especulado (SEO)/*Melanitta fusca deglandi*[4]	LC	-	VR	-	V	-	P
28.	☐ **Bufflehead**/Pato Moñudo/*Bucephala albeola*	LC	-	VR	-	V	-	P
29.	☐ **Hooded Merganser**/Pato de Cresta/*Lophodytes cucullatus*	LC	-	R	-	WR	-	P
30.	☐ **Common Merganser (North American)**/Pato Serrucho Raro/*Mergus merganser americanus*	LC	-	VR	-	V	-	P

	English Name/ Cuban Common Name (CCN)/ *Latin Name*	Threat status	End. Reg.	Abun. status	Breed status	Resid. status	Int.	Dist.
31.	☐ **Red-breasted Merganser**/Pato Serrucho/*Mergus serrator*	LC	-	FC	-	WR-T	-	PC
32.	☐ **Masked Duck**/Pato Agostero/*Nomonyx dominicus*	LC/VU	-	U	Br	YR	-	PC
33.	☐ **Ruddy Duck (Ruddy)**/Pato Chorizo/*Oxyura jamaicensis*	LC	-	FC	Br	PM[W]	-	PC
	Order: GALLIFORMES Family: Numididae							
34.	☐ **Helmeted Guineafowl**/Gallina de Guinea/*Numida meleagris galeatus*	LC	-	FC	Br	YR	C1	PC
	Order: GALLIFORMES Family: Odontophoridae							
35.	☐ **Northern Bobwhite (Eastern)**/Codorniz/*Colinus virginianus cubanensis*[5]	NT	CU	FC	Br	YR	-?	PC
	Order: GALLIFORMES Family: Phasianidae							
36.	☐ **Ring-necked Pheasant (Ring-necked)**/Faisán/*Phasianus colchicus ssp.*	LC	-	U	Br	YR	C1	L
	Order: PHOENICOPTERIFORMES Family: Phoenicopteridae							
37.	☐ **American Flamingo**/Flamenco/*Phoenicopterus ruber*	LC	-	Co	Br	PM	-	QC
	Order: PODICIPEDIFORMES Family: Podicipedidae							
38.	☐ **Least Grebe**/Zaramagullón Chico/*Tachybaptus dominicus dominicus*	LC	-	FC	Br	YR	-	PC
39.	☐ **Pied-billed Grebe**/Zaramagullón Grande/*Podilymbus podiceps podiceps*	LC	-	R	-	WR	-	P
	☐ *Podilymbus podiceps antillarum*	LC	WI	FC	Br	YR	-	PC
	Order: COLUMBIFORMES Family: Columbidae							
40.	☐ **Rock Pigeon (Feral Pigeon)**/Paloma Doméstica/*Columba livia*	LC	-	Co	Br	YR	C4	PC
41.	☐ **Scaly-naped Pigeon**/Torcaza Cuellimorada/*Patagioenas squamosa*	LC	WI	FC	Br	YR	-	PC
42.	☐ **White-crowned Pigeon**/Torcaza Cabeciblanca/*Patagioenas leucocephala*	NT/VU	-	Co	Br	PM	-	PC
43.	☐ **Plain Pigeon**/Torcaza Boba/*Patagioenas inornata inornata*[6]	NT/VU	GA	U	Br	YR	-	L
44.	☐ **Eurasian Collared-Dove**/Tórtola de Collar/*Streptopelia decaocto decaocto*[7]	LC	-	Co	Br	YR	C1	PC
45.	☐ **Passenger Pigeon**/Paloma Migratoria/*Ectopistes migratorius*	Ex	-	†	-	WR	-	†
46.	☐ **Common Ground-Dove**/Tojosa/*Columbina passerina insularis*	LC	GA	Co	Br	YR	-	PC
47.	☐ **Blue-headed Quail-Dove**/Paloma Perdiz/*Starnoenas cyanocephala*	EN	CU	U	Br	YR	-	CC
48.	☐ **Ruddy Quail-Dove (Ruddy)**/Boyero/*Geotrygon montana montana*	LC	-	FC	Br	YR	-	PC
49.	☐ **Gray-fronted Quail-Dove**/Camao/*Geotrygon caniceps*	VU	CU	U	Br	YR	-	QC
50.	☐ **Key West Quail-Dove**/Barbiquejo/*Geotrygon chrysia*	LC	-	FC	Br	YR	-	PC
51.	☐ **White-winged Dove**/Paloma Aliblanca/*Zenaida asiatica asiatica*	LC	-	Co	Br	YR	-	PC
52.	☐ **Zenaida Dove**/Guanaro/*Zenaida aurita zenaida*	LC	GA	Co	Br	YR	-	PC
53.	☐ **Mourning Dove (Caribbean)**/Paloma Rabiche/*Zenaida macroura macroura*	LC	GA	Co	Br	YR	-	PC

		Threat status	End. Reg.	Abun. status	Breed status	Resid. status	Int.	Dist.
	☐ **(Mainland)**/*Zenaida macroura carolinensis*	LC	-	U	-	WR		QC
	English Name/ Cuban Common Name (CCN)/ *Latin Name*	Threat status	End. Reg.	Abun. status	Breed status	Resid. status	Int.	Dist.
	Order: CUCULIFORMES Family: Cuculidae							
54.	☐ **Yellow-billed Cuckoo**/Primavera/*Coccyzus americanus*	LC	-	FC	Br	SR-T	-	PC
55.	☐ **Mangrove Cuckoo**/Arrierito/*Coccyzus minor*	LC	-	FC	Br	YR	-	PC
56.	☐ **Black-billed Cuckoo**/Primavera de Pico Negro/*Coccyzus erythropthalmus*	LC	-	R	-	T	-	P
57.	☐ **Great Lizard-Cuckoo (Cuban)**/Arriero o Guacaica/*Coccyzus merlini[8] merlini*	LC	CU	Co	Br	YR	-	PC
	☐ *Coccyzus merlini santamariae*	LC	CU	Co	Br	YR	-	L
	☐ *Coccyzus merlini decolor*	LC	CU	Co	Br	YR	-	L
58.	☐ **Smooth-billed Ani**/Judío/*Crotophaga ani*	LC	-	Co	Br	YR	-	PC
	Order: CAPRIMULGIFORMES Family: Caprimulgidae							
59.	☐ **Common Nighthawk**/Querequeté Americano/*Chordeiles minor minor*	LC	-	R	-	T	-	P
	☐ *Chordeiles minor howelli*	LC	-	VR	-	T	-	P
60.	☐ **Antillean Nighthawk**/Querequeté/*Chordeiles gundlachii gundlachii[9]*	LC	-	Co	Br	SR	-	PC
61.	☐ **Chuck-will's-widow**/Guabairo Americano/*Antrostomus carolinensis*	LC	-	U	-	WR-T	-	PC
62.	☐ **Cuban Nightjar**/Guabairo/*Antrostomus cubanensis cubanensis*	LC	CU	FC	Br	YR	-	PC
	☐ *Antrostomus cubanensis insulaepinorum*	LC	CU	FC	Br	YR	-	L
63.	☐ **Eastern Whip-poor-will**/Guabairo Chico/*Antrostomus vociferus*	LC	-	R	-	V	-	P
	Order: NYCTIBIIFORMES Family: Nictibiidae							
64.	☐ **Northern Potoo (Caribbean)**/Potú/*Nyctibius jamaicensis ssp.[10]*	LC	?	R	?	YR?	-	P
	Order: APODIFORMES Family: Apodidae[11]							
65.	☐ **Black Swift (niger)**/Vencejo Negro/*Cypseloides niger niger*	LC	WI	U	Br	YR	-	L
66.	☐ **White-collared Swift**/Vencejo de Collar/*Streptoprocne zonaris pallidifrons*	LC	WI	U	Br	YR	-	L
67.	☐ **Chimney Swift**/Vencejo de Chimenea/*Chaetura pelagica*	NT	-	R	-	T	-	P
68.	☐ **Antillean Palm-Swift**/Vencejito de Palma/*Tachornis phoenicobia iradii*	LC	CU	Co	Br	YR	-	PC
	Order: APODIFORMES Family: Trochilidae[12]							
69.	☐ **Bahama Woodstar**/Colibrí de Bahamas/*Calliphlox evelynae[13]*	LC	LY	VR	-	V	-	P
70.	☐ **Ruby-throated Hummingbird**/Colibrí de Garganta Rubí/*Archilochus colubris*	LC	-	R	-	T	-	P
71.	☐ **Bee Hummingbird**/ Zunzuncito/*Mellisuga helenae*	NT/VU	CU	U	Br	YR	-	QC
72.	☐ **Cuban Emerald**/Zunzún/*Chlorostilbon ricordii[14]*	LC	CU-LY	Co	Br	YR	-	PC
	Order: GRUIFORMES Family: Rallidae							
73.	☐ **Black Rail (Northern)**/Gallinuelita Prieta/*Laterallus jamaicensis jamaicensis*	NT	-	R	Br	PM[W]	-	QC
74.	☐ **Clapper Rail (Caribbean)**/Gallinuela de Manglar/*Rallus crepitans caribaeus*	LC	WI	FC	Br	YR	-	QC

	English Name/ Cuban Common Name (CCN)/ *Latin Name*	Threat status	End. Reg.	Abun. status	Breed status	Resid. status	Int.	Dist.
	☐ (Atlantic Coast)/*Rallus crepitans crepitans*	LC	-	VR	-	V	-	P
75.	☐ **King Rail (Cuban)**/Gallinuela de Agua Dulce/*Rallus elegans ramsdeni*	NT	CU	FC	Br	YR	-	QC
	☐ *Rallus elegans elegans*[a]	NT	-	VR	-	V	-	P
76.	☐ **Virginia Rail (Virginia)**/Gallinuela de Virginia/*Rallus limicola limicola*	LC	-	VR	-	V	-	P
77.	☐ **Sora**/ Gallinuela Oscura/ *Porzana carolina*	LC	-	FC	-	WR-T	-	QC
78.	☐ **Yellow-breasted Crake**/Gallinuelita/*Hapalocrex flaviventer gossii*	LC	GA	U	Br	YR	-	L
79.	☐ **Zapata Rail**/Gallinuela de Santo Tomás/*Cyanolimnas cerverai*[15]	CR	CU	XR	Br	YR	-	L
80.	☐ **Spotted Rail**/Gallinuela Escribano/*Pardirallus maculatus maculatus*[16]	LC	-	FC	Br	YR	-	QC
81.	☐ **Purple Gallinule**/Gallareta Azul/*Porphyrio martinicus*	LC	-	Co	Br	PM	-	PC
82.	☐ **Common Gallinule (American)**/Gallareta de Pico Rojo/*Gallinula galeata cerceris*	LC	WI	Co	Br	PM	-	PC
83.	☐ **American Coot**/Gallareta de Pico Blanco/*Fulica americana*[17]	LC	-	Co	Br	PM	-	PC
	Order: GRUIFORMES Family: Aramidae							
84.	☐ **Limpkin (Speckled)**/Guareao/*Aramus guarauna pictus*	LC	-	Co	Br	YR	-	PC
	Order: GRUIFORMES Family: Gruidae							
85.	☐ **Sandhill Crane (nesiotes)**/Grulla/*Antigone canadensis nesiotes*	LC/VU	CU	U	Br	YR	-	Rg
	Order: CHARADRIIFORMES Family: Recurvirostridae							
86.	☐ **Black-necked Stilt (Black-necked)**/Cachiporra/*Himantopus mexicanus mexicanus*	LC	-	Co	Br	PM	-	PC
87.	☐ **American Avocet**/Avoceta Americana/*Recurvirostra americana*	LC	-	U	Br[18]	PM^W	-	QC
	Order: CHARADRIIFORMES Family: Haematopodidae							
88.	☐ **American Oystercatcher**/Ostrero/*Haematopus palliatus palliatus*	LC	-	R	Br[19]	PM^W	-	QC
	Order: CHARADRIIFORMES Family: Charadriidae							
89.	☐ **Black-bellied Plover**/Pluvial Cabezón/*Pluvialis squatarola squatarola*	LC	-	Co	?	PM^W20	-	QC
90.	☐ **American Golden-Plover**/Pluvial Dorado/*Pluvialis dominica*	LC	-	R	-	T	-	P
91.	☐ **Snowy Plover (nivosus)**/Frailecillo Blanco/*Charadrius nivosus nivosus*	NT/VU	-	U	Br	PM^W21	-	QC
92.	☐ **Wilson's Plover**/Titere Playero/*Charadrius wilsonia wilsonia*	LC	-	Co	Br	PM^S22	-	PC
93.	☐ **Semipalmated Plover**/Frailecillo Semipalmeado/*Charadrius semipalmatus*	LC	-	Co	-	WR-T	-	QC
94.	☐ **Piping Plover**/Frailecillo Silbador/*Charadrius melodus melodus*	NT/VU	-	U	-	WR-T	-	QC
95.	☐ **Killdeer**/Títere Sabanero/*Charadrius vociferus vociferus*	LC	-	FC	-	WR	-	PC
	☐ *Charadrius vociferus ternominatus*	LC	GA	Co	Br	YR	-	PC
	Order: CHARADRIIFORMES Family: Jacanidae							
96.	☐ **Northern Jacana**/Gallito de Río/*Jacana spinosa violacea*	LC	GA	Co	Br	YR	-	PC

	English Name/ Cuban Common Name (CCN)/ *Latin Name*	Threat status	End. Reg.	Abun. status	Breed status	Resid. status	Int.	Dist.
	Order: CHARADRIIFORMES Family: Scolopacidae							
97.	☐ **Upland Sandpiper**/Ganga/*Bartramia longicauda*	LC	-	R	-	T	-	P
98.	☐ **Whimbrel (Hudsonian)**/Zarapico Pico de Cimitarra Chico/*Numenius phaeopus hudsonicus*[23]	LC	-	U	-	WR-T	-	P
99.	☐ **Long-billed Curlew**/Zarapico Pico de Cimitarra Grande/*Numenius americanus americanus*	LC	-	R	-	V	-	P
100.	☐ **Hudsonian Godwit**/Avoceta Pechirroja/*Limosa haemastica*	LC	-	R	-	V	-	P
101.	☐ **Marbled Godwit**/Avoceta Parda/*Limosa fedoa fedoa*	LC	-	R	-	V	-	P
102.	☐ **Ruddy Turnstone**/Revuelvepiedras/*Arenaria interpres morinella*	LC	-	Co	?	PM[W24]	-	PC
103.	☐ **Red Knot**/Zarapico Raro/*Calidris canutus ssp.*	NT	-	FC	-	WR[25]-T	-	P
104.	☐ **Ruff**/Combatiente (SEO)/*Calidris pugnax*	LC	-	VR	-	V	-	P
105.	☐ **Stilt Sandpiper**/Zarapico Patilargo/*Calidris himantopus*	LC	-	FC	-	WR	-	QC
106.	☐ **Curlew Sandpiper**/Correlimos Zarapitín (SEO)/*Calidirs ferruginea*[b]	NT	-	VR	-	WR?	-	P
107.	☐ **Sanderling**/Zarapico Blanco/*Calidris alba*[26]	LC	-	Co	-	WR-T	-	PC
108.	☐ **Dunlin**/Zarapico Gris/*Calidris alpina (prob. hudsonia)*	LC	-	R	-	WR-T	-	P
109.	☐ **Least Sandpiper**/Zarapiquito/*Calidris minutilla*	LC	-	Co	-	WR-T	-	QC
110.	☐ **White-rumped Sandpiper**/Zarapico de Rabadilla Blanca/*Calidris fuscicollis*	LC	-	U	-	T	-	P
111.	☐ **Buff-breasted Sandpiper**/Zarapico Piquicorto/*Calidris subruficollis*	NT	-	VR	-	V	-	P
112.	☐ **Pectoral Sandpiper**/Zarapico Moteado/*Calidris melanotos*	LC	-	FC	-	T	-	P
113.	☐ **Semipalmated Sandpiper**/Zarapico Semipalmeado/*Calidris pusilla*	NT	-	FC	-	WR-T	-	QC
114.	☐ **Western Sandpiper**/Zarapico Chico/*Calidris mauri*	LC	-	FC	-	WR?-T	-	QC
115.	☐ **Short-billed Dowitcher (griseus)**/Zarapico Becasina/*Limnodromus griseus griseus*	LC	-	Co	-	WR-T	-	QC
116.	☐ **Long-billed Dowitcher**/Zarapico Becasina de Pico Largo/*Limnodromus scolopaceus*	LC	-	FC	-	WR-T	-	QC
117.	☐ **Wilson's Snipe**/Becasina/*Gallinago delicata*	LC	-	FC	-	WR-T	-	PC
118.	☐ **Spotted Sandpiper**/Zarapico Manchado/*Actitis macularius*	LC	-	Co	-	WR-T	-	PC
119.	☐ **Solitary Sandpiper (solitaria)**/Zarapico Solitario/*Tringa solitaria solitaria*	LC	-	FC	-	WR-T	-	QC
120.	☐ **Greater Yellowlegs**/Zarapico Patiamarillo Grande/*Tringa melanoleuca*	LC	-	Co	?	PM[W27]	-	PC
121.	☐ **Lesser Yellowlegs**/Zarapico Patiamarillo Chico/*Tringa flavipes*	LC	-	Co	?	PM[W28]	-	PC
122.	☐ **Willet (Eastern)**/Zarapico Real/*Tringa semipalmata semipalmata*	LC	-	Co	Br	PM[W]	-	PC
	☐ **Western**/*Tringa semipalmata inornata*[29]	LC	-	VR	-	V	-	P
123.	☐ **Wilson's Phalarope**/Zarapico de Wilson/ *Phalaropus tricolor*[30]	LC	-	R	-	V	-	P
124.	☐ **Red-necked Phalarope**/Zarapico Nadador/*Phalaropus lobatus*	LC	-	VR	-	V	-	P
125.	☐ **Red Phalarope**/Zarapico Rojo/*Phalaropus fulicarius*	LC	-	VR	-	V	-	P

	English Name/ Cuban Common Name (CCN)/ *Latin Name*	Threat status	End. Reg.	Abun. status	Breed status	Resid. status	Int.	Dist.
	Order: CHARADRIIFORMES Family: Stercorariidae							
126.	☐ **South Polar Skua**/Skua del Polo Sur/*Stercorarius maccormicki*	LC	-	VR	-	V	-	P
127.	☐ **Pomarine Jaeger**/Estercorario Pomarino/*Stercorarius pomarinus*	LC	-	VR	-	V	-	P
128.	☐ **Parasitic Jaeger**/Estercorario Parasítico/*Stercorarius parasiticus*	LC	-	R	-	V	-	P
129.	☐ **Long-tailed Jaeger**/Estercorario Rabero/*Stercorarius longicaudus pallescens*	LC	-	VR	-	V	-	P
	Order: CHARADRIIFORMES Family: Alcidae							
130.	☐ **Dovekie**/Pingüinito/*Alle alle alle*	LC	-	R	-	V	-	P
	Order: CHARADRIIFORMES Family: Laridae							
131.	☐ **Black-legged Kittiwake (tridactyla)**/Gallego Patinegro/*Rissa tridactyla tridactyla*	LC	-	R	-	V	-	P
132.	☐ **Sabine's Gull**/Gallego de Cola Ahorquillada/*Xema sabini sabini*	LC	-	VR	-	V	-	P
133.	☐ **Bonaparte's Gull**/Galleguito Chico/*Chroicocephalus philadelphia*	LC	-	R	-	WR-T[31]	-	P
134.	☐ **Black-headed Gull**/Galleguito Raro/*Chroicocephalus ridibundus*	LC	-	VR	-	V	-	P
135.	☐ **Laughing Gull**/Galleguito/*Leucophaeus atricilla atricilla*	LC	-	Co	Br	PM[W]	-	PC
136.	☐ **Franklin´s Gull**/Galleguito de Franklin/*Leucophaeus pipixcan*	LC	-	VR	-	V	-	P
137.	☐ **Ring-billed Gull**/Gallego Real/*Larus delawarensis*	LC	-	FC	-	WR-T	-	P
138.	☐ **Herring Gull (American)**/Gallego/*Larus argentatus smithsonianus*[32]	LC	-	Co	-	WR-T	-	QC
139.	☐ **Lesser Black-backed Gull**/Gallego Pequeño de Espalda Negra/*Larus fuscus* (prob. *graellsii*)	LC	-	R	-	WR	-	P
140.	☐ **Great Black-backed Gull**/Gallegón/*Larus marinus*	LC	-	VR	-	WR	-	P
141.	☐ **Brown Noddy**/Gaviota Boba/*Anous stolidus stolidus*	LC	-	FC	Br	SR-T[33]	-	QC
142.	☐ **Sooty Tern**/Gaviota Monja Prieta/*Onychoprion fuscatus fuscatus*	LC	-	U	Br	PM[S]	-	L
143.	☐ **Bridled Tern**/Gaviota Monja/*Onychoprion anaethetus recognitus*[34]	LC	-	Co	Br	SR	-	L
144.	☐ **Least Tern**/Gaviotica/*Sternula antillarum antillarum*	LC	-	Co	Br	PM[35]	-	QC
145.	☐ **Large-billed Tern**/Gaviota de Pico Largo/*Phaetusa simplex simplex*	LC	-	VR	-	V	-	P
146.	☐ **Gull-billed Tern (Gull-billed)**/Gaviota de Pico Corto/ *Gelochelidon nilotica aranea*	LC	-	U	-	PM[W36]	-	PC
147.	☐ **Caspian Tern**/Gaviota Real Grande/*Hydroprogne caspia*	LC	-	FC	?	PM[W37]	-	QC
148.	☐ **Black Tern (American)**/Gaviotica Prieta/*Chlidonias niger surinamensis*	LC	-	R	-	T	-	QC
149.	☐ **Roseate Tern**/Gaviota Rosada/*Sterna dougallii dougallii*	LC/ VU	-	R	Br[38]	PM[S]	-	P
150.	☐ **Common Tern (hirundo)**/Gaviota Común/*Sterna hirundo hirundo*	LC	-	U	-	PM[W39]	-	PC
151.	☐ **Arctic Tern**/Gaviota Ártica/*Sterna paradisaea*	LC	-	VR	-	V	-	P
152.	☐ **Forster's Tern**/Gaviota de Forster/*Sterna forsteri*	LC	-	R	-	WR	-	P

English Name/ Cuban Common Name (CCN)/ *Latin Name*	Threat status	End. Reg.	Abun. status	Breed status	Resid. status	Int.	Dist.
153. ☐ **Royal Tern (American)**/Gaviota Real/*Thalasseus maximus maximus*	LC	-	Co	Br	PM^W	-	PC
154. ☐ **Sandwich Tern (Cabot´s)**/Gaviota de Pico Amarillo/*Thalasseus sandvicensis acuflavidus*	LC	-	FC	Br	PM^S	-	QC
☐ **(Cayenne)**/*Thalasseus sandvicensis eurygnatus*[40]	LC	-	VR	Br	SR-T	-	L
155. ☐ **Black Skimmer (niger)**/Gaviota Pico de Tijera/*Rynchops niger niger*	LC	-	FC	-	WR-T	-	QC
Order: PHAETHONTIFORMES Family: Phaethontidae							
156. ☐ **White-tailed Tropicbird (Atlantic)**/Contramaestre/*Phaethon lepturus catesbyi*	LC	-	U	Br	SR	-	L
157. ☐ **Red-billed Tropicbird**/Rabijunco de Pico Rojo/*Phaethon aethereus mesonauta*	LC	-	R	-	V	-	P
Order: GAVIIFORMES Family: Gaviidae							
158. ☐ **Common Loon**/Somormujo/*Gavia immer*	LC	-	R	-	V	-	P
Order: PROCELLARIIFORMES Family: Oceanitidae[41]							
159. ☐ **Wilson's Storm-Petrel (Wilson´s)**/Pamperito de Wilson/*Oceanites oceanicus oceanicus*	LC	-	R	-	V	-	P
Order: PROCELLARIIFORMES Family: Hydrobatidae							
160. ☐ **Leach's Storm-Petrel (Leach´s)**/Pamperito de las Tempestades/*Oceanodroma*[42] *leucorhoa*	VU	-	VR	-	V	-	P
161. ☐ **Band-rumped Storm-Petrel**/Pamperito de Castro/*Oceanodroma*[43] *castro*	LC	-	VR	-	V	-	P
Order: PROCELLARIIFORMES Family: Procellariidae							
162. ☐ **Black-capped Petrel**/Pájaro de las Brujas/*Pterodroma hasitata*	EN	-	VR	Br?	SR?	-	L
163. ☐ **Cory's Shearwater (borealis)**/Pampero de Cory/*Calonectris diomedea borealis*[44]	LC	-	R	-	V	-	P
164. ☐ **Sooty Shearwater**/Pampero Oscuro/*Ardenna grisea*	NT	-	R	-	V	-	P
165. ☐ **Great Shearwater**/Pampero Grande/*Ardenna gravis*	LC	-	VR	-	V	-	P
166. ☐ **Audubon's Shearwater**/Pampero de Audubon/*Puffinus iherminieri iherminieri*	LC	-	R	Br[45]	YR-PM?	-	P
Order: CICONIIFORMES Family: Ciconiidae							
167. ☐ **Wood Stork**/Cayama/*Mycteria americana*	LC	-	U	Br	YR	-	L
Order: SULIFORMES Family: Fregatidae							
168. ☐ **Magnificent Frigatebird**/Rabiahorcado/*Fregata magnificens*[46]	LC	-	Co	Br	YR	-	PC
Order: SULIFORMES Family: Sulidae							
169. ☐ **Masked Booby**/Pájaro Bobo de Cara Azul/*Sula dactylatra dactylatra*	LC	-	R	-	V	-	P
170. ☐ **Brown Booby (Atlantic)**/Pájaro Bobo Prieto/*Sula leucogaster leucogaster*	LC	-	R	Br	YR	-	P
171. ☐ **Red-footed Booby (Atlantic)**/Pájaro Bobo Blanco/*Sula sula sula*	LC	-	R	-	V	-	P
172. ☐ **Northern Gannet**/Albatros/*Morus bassanus*	LC	-	VR	-	V	-	P

	English Name/ Cuban Common Name (CCN)/ *Latin Name*	Threat status	End. Reg.	Abun. status	Breed status	Resid. status	Int.	Dist.
	Order: SULIFORMES Family: Phalacrocoracidae							
173.	☐ **Neotropic Cormorant**/Corúa de Agua Dulce/*Phalacrocorax brasilianus mexicanus*	LC	-	Co	Br	YR	-	PC
174.	☐ **Double-crested Cormorant**/Corúa de Mar/*Phalacrocorax auritus auritus*	LC	-	Co	Br	YR	-	PC
	☐ *Phalacrocorax auritus floridanus*	LC	-	VR	-	V	-	P
	Order: SULIFORMES Family: Anhingidae							
175.	☐ **Anhinga**/Marbella/*Anhinga anhinga leucogaster*	LC	-	Co	Br	YR	-	PC
	Order: PELECANIFORMES Family: Pelecanidae							
176.	☐ **American White Pelican**/Pelícano Blanco/*Pelecanus erythrorhynchos*	LC	-	FC	-	PM[W47]	-	QC
177.	☐ **Brown Pelican (Southern)**/Pelícano/*Pelecanus occidentalis occidentalis*	LC	-	Co	Br	YR	-	QC
	☐ **(Atlantic)**/*Pelecanus occidentalis carolinensis*	LC	-	FC	?	PM?		PC
	Order: PELECANIFORMES Family: Ardeidae							
178.	☐ **American Bittern**/Guanabá Rojo/*Botaurus lentiginosus*	LC	-	U	-	WR-T[48]	-	QC
179.	☐ **Least Bittern**/Garcita/*Ixobrychus exilis exilis*	LC	-	FC	Br	PM	-	PC
180.	☐ **Great Blue Heron**/Garcilote Azul/*Ardea herodias herodias*	LC	-	Co	Br	PM	-	PC
	☐ *Ardea herodias occidentalis*[49]	LC	-	U	?	?	-	P
181.	☐ **Great Egret (American)**/Garzón/*Ardea alba egretta*	LC	-	Co	Br	PM	-	PC
182.	☐ **Snowy Egret**/Garza Real/*Egretta thula thula*	LC	-	Co	Br	PM	-	PC
183.	☐ **Little Blue Heron**/Garza Azul/*Egretta caerulea*	LC	-	Co	Br	PM	-	PC
184.	☐ **Tricolored Heron**/Garza de Vientre Blanco/*Egretta tricolor ruficollis*	LC	-	Co	Br	PM	-	PC
185.	☐ **Reddish Egret**/Garza Rojiza/*Egretta rufescens rufescens*	NT	-	FC	Br	PM	-	QC
186.	☐ **Cattle Egret (Western)**/Garcita Bueyera/*Bubulcus ibis ibis*	LC	-	Co	Br	PM	-	PC
187.	☐ **Green Heron (virescens/bahamensis)**/Aguaitacaimán/*Butorides virescens virescens*[50]	LC	-	Co	Br	PM	-	PC
188.	☐ **Black-crowned Night-Heron (American)**/Guanabá de la Florida/*Nycticorax nycticorax hoactli*	LC	-	Co	Br	PM	-	PC
189.	☐ **Yellow-crowned Night-Heron (violacea Group)**/Guanabá Real/*Nyctanassa violacea violacea*	LC	-	U	-	WR-T	-	QC
	☐ *Nyctanassa violacea bancrofti*	LC	-	Co	Br	PM	-	PC
	Order: PELECANIFORMES Family: Threskiornithidae							
190.	☐ **White Ibis**/Coco Blanco/*Eudocimus albus*[51]	LC	-	Co	Br	PM	-	PC
191.	☐ **Scarlet Ibis**/Coco Rojo/*Eudocimus ruber*[52]	LC	-	VR	-	V	-	P
192.	☐ **Glossy Ibis**/Coco Prieto/*Plegadis falcinellus*[53]	LC	-	Co	Br	PM	-	PC
193.	☐ **Roseate Spoonbill**/Sevilla/*Platalea ajaja*	LC	-	Co	Br	YR	-	PC
	Order: CATHARTIFORMES[54] Family: Cathartidae							
194.	☐ **Black Vulture**/Zopilote/*Coragyps atratus atratus*	LC	-	R	?	PM[55]	-	L
195.	☐ **Turkey Vulture (Northern)**/Aura Tiñosa/*Cathartes aura aura*	LC	-	Co	Br	PM	-	PC

English Name/ Cuban Common Name (CCN)/ *Latin Name*	Threat status	End. Reg.	Abun. status	Breed status	Resid. status	Int.	Dist.
Order: ACCIPITRIFORMES Family: Pandionidae							
196. ☐ Osprey (***carolinensis***)/Guincho/*Pandion haliaetus carolinensis*	LC	-	Co	-[56]	WR	-	PC
☐ (***ridgwayi***)/*Pandion haliaetus ridgwayi*	LC	-	U	Br	YR	-	L
Order: ACCIPITRIFORMES Family: Accipitridae							
197. ☐ **Cuban Kite**/Gavilán Caguarero/*Chondrohierax wilsonii*[57]	CR	CU	XR	Br	YR	-	L
198. ☐ **Swallow-tailed Kite**/Gavilán Cola de Tijera/*Elanoides forficatus forficatus*	LC	-	FC	-	T	-	QC
199. ☐ **Northern Harrier**/Gavilán Sabanero/*Circus hudsonicus*	LC	-	FC	-	WR-T	-	PC
200. ☐ **Sharp-shinned Hawk (Northern)**/Gavilancito/*Accipiter striatus velox*	LC	-	FC	-	WR-T	-	PC
☐ **(Caribbean)**/*Accipiter striatus fringilloides*	LC	CU	U	-	YR	-	PC
201. ☐ **Cooper's Hawk**/Gavilán de Cooper/*Accipiter cooperi*	LC	-	VR	-	T	-	P
202. ☐ **Gundlach's Hawk**/Gavilán Colilargo/*Accipiter gundlachi gundlachi*	EN	CU	U	Br	YR	-	CC
☐ *Accipiter gundlachi wileyi*	EN	CU	U	Br	YR	-	Rg
203. ☐ **Bald Eagle**/Águila Calva/*Haliaeetus leucocephalus leucocephalus*	LC	-	R	-	V	-	P
204. ☐ **Mississippi Kite**/Gavilán del Mississippi/*Ictinia mississippiensis*	LC	-	FC	-	T	-	P
205. ☐ **Snail Kite**/Gavilán Caracolero/*Rostrhamus sociabilis plumbeus*	LC	-	FC	Br	YR	-	PC
206. ☐ **Cuban Black Hawk**/Gavilán Batista/*Buteogallus gundlachii*	NT/EN	CU	FC	Br	YR	-	QC
207. ☐ **Broad-winged Hawk (Northern)**/Gavilán Bobo/*Buteo platypterus platypterus*	LC	-	VR	-	WR-T	-	P
☐ **(Caribbean)**/*Buteo platypterus cubanensis*	LC	CU	Co	Br	YR	-	PC
208. ☐ **Short-tailed Hawk**/Gavilán de Cola Corta/*Buteo brachyurus* (prob. *fuliginosus*)	LC	-	R	-	T	-	P
209. ☐ **Swainson's Hawk**/Gavilán de Swainson/*Buteo swainsoni*	LC	-	R	-	T	-	P
210. ☐ **Red-tailed Hawk**/Gavilán de Monte/*Buteo jamaicensis solitudinis*	LC	CU/LY	Co	Br	YR	-	PC
Order: STRIGIFORMES Family: Tytonidae							
211. ☐ **Barn Owl (American)**/Lechuza/*Tyto alba pranticola*	LC	-	VR	-	V	-	P
☐ *Tyto alba furcata*	LC	GA	Co	Br	YR	-	PC
☐ *Tyto alba niveicauda*	LC	CU	Co	Br	YR	-	L
Order: STRIGIFORMES Family: Strigidae							
212. ☐ **Bare-legged Owl**/Sijú Cotunto/*Margarobyas lawrencii lawrencii*	LC	CU	FC	Br	YR	-	PC
☐ *Margarobyas lawrencii exsul*[58]	LC	CU	FC	Br	YR	-	L
213. ☐ **Cuban Pygmy-Owl**/Sijú Platanero/*Glaucidium siju siju*	LC	CU	Co	Br	YR	-	PC
☐ *Glaucidium siju vitatum*	LC	CU	Co	Br	YR	-	L
☐ *Glaucidium siju turquinensis*	LC	CU	Co	Br	YR	-	L
214. ☐ **Burrowing Owl (Florida)**/Sijú de Sabana/*Athene cunicularia*[59] *floridana*	LC	-	R	-	WR	-	P
☐ *Athene cunicularia guantanamensis*	LC	CU	U	Br	YR	-	L

	English Name/ Cuban Common Name (CCN)/ *Latin Name*	Threat status	End. Reg.	Abun. status	Breed status	Resid. status	Int.	Dist.
215.	☐ **Long-eared Owl (American)**/Buho Chico (SEO)/*Asio otus wilsonianus*	LC	-	VR	-	V	-	P
216.	☐ **Stygian Owl**/Siguapa/*Asio stygius siguapa*	LC	CU	U	Br	YR	-	PC
217.	☐ **Short-eared Owl (Antillean)**/Cárabo/*Asio flammeus dominguensis*[60]	LC	GA	FC	Br	YR	-	PC
	Order: TROGONIFORMES Family: Trogonidae							
218.	☐ **Cuban Trogon**/Tocororo/*Priotelus temnurus temnurus*	LC	CU	Co	Br	YR	-	PC
	☐ *Priotelus temnurus vescus*	LC	CU	Co	Br	YR	-	L
	Order: CORACIIFORMES Family: Todidae							
219.	☐ **Cuban Tody**/Cartacuba/*Todus multicolor*	LC	CU	Co	Br	YR	-	PC
	Order: CORACIIFORMES Family: Alcedinidae							
220.	☐ **Belted Kingfisher**/Martín Pescador/*Megaceryle alcyon*	LC	-	Co	-	WR-T	-	PC
	Order: PICIFORMES Family: Picidae							
221.	☐ **West Indian Woodpecker**/Carpintero Jabado/*Melanerpes superciliaris superciliaris*[61]	LC	GA	Co	Br	YR	-	PC
	☐ *Melanerpes superciliaris murceus*	LC	CU	Co	Br	YR	-	L
222.	☐ **Yellow-bellied Sapsucker**/Carpintero de Paso/*Sphyrapicus varius*	LC	-	FC	-	WR-T	-	PC
223.	☐ **Cuban Green Woodpecker**/Carpintero Verde/*Xiphidiopicus percussus percussus*[62]	LC	CU	Co	Br	YR	-	PC
	☐ *Xiphidiopicus percussus insulaepinorum*	LC	CU	Co	Br	YR	-	L
224.	☐ **Northern Flicker (Cuban)** /Carpintero Escapulario/*Colaptes auratus chrysocaulosus*[63]	LC	CU	FC	Br	YR	-	PC
225.	☐ **Fernandina's Flicker**/Carpintero Churroso/*Colaptes fernandinae*	VU	CU	U	Br	YR	-	QC
226.	☐ **Ivory-billed Woodpecker (Cuban)** /Carpintero Real/*Campephilus principalis bairdii*[64]	CR-EX?	CU	XR	Br	YR	-	L
	Order: FALCONIFORMES Family: Falconidae							
227.	☐ **Crested Caracara**/Caraira/*Caracara cheriway audubonii*[65]	LC	-	FC	Br	YR	-	QC
228.	☐ **American Kestrel (Northern)**/Cernícalo/*Falco sparverius sparverius*	LC	-	Co	-	WR-T	-	PC
	☐ **(Cuban)**/*Falco sparverius sparverioides*[66]	LC	GA	Co	Br	YR	-	PC
229.	☐ **Merlin (Taiga)**/Halcón de Palomas/*Falco columbarius columbarius*	LC	-	Co	-	WR-T	-	PC
230.	☐ **Peregrine Falcon (North American)**/Halcón Peregrino/*Falco peregrinus anatum*	LC	-	FC	Br?	WR-T	-	PC
	☐ **(tundrius)**/*Falco peregrinus tundrius*	LC	-	R	-	V-T	-	P
	Order: PSITTACIFORMES Family: Psittacidae							
231.	☐ **Red-and-green Macaw**/Guacamayo Rojo y Azul/*Ara chloropterus*[67]	LC	-	U	Br	YR	C1	L
232.	☐ **Scarlet Macaw**/Guacamayo Rojo/*Ara macao ssp.*[68]	LC	-	U	Br	YR	C1	L
233.	☐ **Cuban Macaw**/Guacamayo Cubano/*Ara tricolor*	Ex	CU	†	†	†	-	†
234.	☐ **Blue-and-yellow Macaw**/Guacamayo Azul y Amarillo/*Ara*	LC	-	U	Br	YR	C1	L

English Name/ Cuban Common Name (CCN)/ *Latin Name*	Threat status	End. Reg.	Abun. status	Breed status	Resid. status	Int.	Dist.
ararauna[69]							
235. ☐ **Cuban Parakeet**/Catey/*Psittacara euops*	VU/EN	CU	U	Br	YR	-	QC
236. ☐ **Cuban Amazon (Cuban)**/Cotorra/*Amazona leucocephala leucocephala*	NT/VU	CU	Co	Br	YR	-	QC
Order: PASSERIFORMES Family: Tyrannidae							
237. ☐ **Great Crested Flycatcher**/Bobito de Cresta/*Myiarchus crinitus*	LC	-	R	-	T	-	P
238. ☐ **La Sagra's Flycatcher**/Bobito Grande/*Myiarchus sagrae sagrae*	LC	CU-CI	Co	Br	YR	-	PC
239. ☐ **Tropical Kingbird**/Pitirre Tropical/*Tyrannus melancholicus satrapa*	LC	-	R	-	V	-	P
240. ☐ **Cassin´s Kingbird**/Pitirre de Cassin/*Tyrannus vociferans vociferans*	LC	-	VR	-	V	-	P
241. ☐ **Western Kingbird**/Pitirre del Oeste/*Tyrannus verticalis*	LC	-	R	-	V	-	P
242. ☐ **Eastern Kingbird**/Pitirre Americano/*Tyrannus tyrannus*	LC	-	U	-	T	-	PC
243. ☐ **Gray Kingbird**/Pitirre Abejero/*Tyrannus dominicensis dominicensis*	LC	-	Co	Br	SR-T	-	PC
244. ☐ **Loggerhead Kingbird (Loggerhead)**/Pitirre Guatíbere/*Tyrannus caudifasciatus caudifasciatus*	LC	CU	Co	Br	YR	-	PC
☐ *Tyrannus caudifasciatus flavescens*	LC	CU	Co	Br	YR	-	L
245. ☐ **Giant Kingbird**/Pitirre Real/*Tyrannus cubensis*[70]	EN	CU/LY †	U	Br	YR	-	QC
246. ☐ **Scissor-tailed Flycatcher**/Bobito Cola de Tijera/*Tyrannus forficatus*	LC	-	R	-	V	-	P
247. ☐ **Fork-tailed Flycatcher**/Pitirre de Cola Ahorquillada/*Tyrannus savana* (prob. *monachus*)	LC	-	VR	-	V	-	P
248. ☐ **Western Wood-Pewee**/Bobito de Bosque del Oeste/*Contopus sordidulus* (prob. *saturatus*)	LC	-	R	-	T	-	P
249. ☐ **Eastern Wood-Pewee**/Bobito de Bosque del Este/*Contopus virens*	LC	-	FC	-	T	-	QC
250. ☐ **Cuban Pewee**/Bobito Chico/*Contopus caribaeus caribaeus*[71]	LC	CU	Co	Br	YR	-	PC
☐ *Contopus caribaeus morenoi*	LC	CU	Co	Br	YR	-	L
☐ *Contopus caribaeus nerlyi*	LC	CU	Co	Br	YR	-	L
251. ☐ **Yellow-bellied Flycatcher**/Bobito Amarillo/*Empidonax flaviventris*	LC	-	R	-	T	-	P
252. ☐ **Acadian Flycatcher**/Bobito Verde/*Empidonax virescens*	LC	-	U	-	T	-	P
253. ☐ **Alder Flycatcher**/Bobito de Alder/*Empidonax alnorum*[72]	LC	-	VR	-	T	-	P
254. ☐ **Willow Flycatcher**/Bobito de Trail/*Empidonax traillii*[73]	LC	-	VR	-	T	-	P
255. ☐ **Least Flycatcher**/Bobito de Least/*Empidonax minimus*[74]	LC	-	VR	-	V	-	P
256. ☐ **Eastern Phoebe**/Bobito Americano/*Sayornis phoebe*	LC	-	R	-	V	-	P
257. ☐ **Vermilion Flycatcher (Northern)**/Bobito Bermellón/*Pyrocephalus rubinus* (prob. *blatteus*)[75]	LC	-	VR	-	V	-	P
Order: PASSERIFORMES Family: Vireonidae							
258. ☐ **White-eyed Vireo (White-eyed)**/Vireo de Ojo Blanco/*Vireo griseus griseus*	LC	-	Co	-	WR-T	-	PC
☐ *Vireo griseus noveboracensis*	LC	-	R	-	WR-T	-	QC

	English Name/ Cuban Common Name (CCN)/ *Latin Name*	Threat status	End. Reg.	Abun. status	Breed status	Resid. status	Int.	Dist.
259.	☐ **Thick-billed Vireo**/Vireo de Bahamas/*Vireo crassirostris cubensis*	VU/LC	CU	U	Br	YR	-	L
260.	☐ **Cuban Vireo**/Juan Chiví/*Vireo gundlachii gundlachii*[76]	LC	CU	Co	Br	YR	-	PC
	☐ *Vireo gundlachii sanfelipensis*	LC	CU	Co	Br	YR	-	L
	☐ *Vireo gundlachii magnus*	LC	CU	Co	Br	YR	-	L
	☐ *Vireo gundlachii orientalis*	LC	CU	Co	Br	YR	-	R
261.	☐ **Yellow-throated Vireo**/Verdón de Pecho Amarillo/*Vireo flavifrons*	LC	-	FC	-	WR-T	-	PC
262.	☐ **Blue-headed Vireo**/Verdón de Cabeza Gris/*Vireo solitarius solitarius*	LC	-	U	-	WR-T	-	PC
263.	☐ **Philadelphia Vireo**/Vireo de Filadelfia/*Vireo philadelphicus*	LC	-	R	-	T	-	P
264.	☐ **Warbling Vireo**/Vireo Cantor/*Vireo gilvus gilvus*	LC	-	R	-	WR-T	-	P
265.	☐ **Red-eyed Vireo**/Vireo de Ojo Rojo/*Vireo olivaceus olivaceus*	LC	-	FC	-	WR-T	-	PC
266.	☐ **Black-whiskered Vireo**/ Bien-te-veo/ *Vireo altiloquus barbatulus*	LC	-	Co	Br	SR-T	-	PC

Order: PASSERIFORMES   Family: Corvidae

267.	☐ **Palm Crow (Cuban)**/Cao Pinalero/*Corvus palmarum minutus*	NT/EN	GA	U	Br	YR	-	L
268.	☐ **Cuban Crow**/Cao Montero/*Corvus nasicus*	LC	CU-LY	FC	Br	YR	-	QC

Order: PASSERIFORMES   Family: Hirundinidae

269.	☐ **Purple Martin (subis/arboricola)**/Golondrina Azul/*Progne subis subis*	LC	-	FC	-	T	-	QC
270.	☐ **Cuban Martin**/Golondrina Azul Cubana/*Progne cryptoleuca*	LC	-	Co	Br	SR	-	PC
271.	☐ **Caribbean Martin**/Golondrina Caribeña/*Progne dominicensis*[c]	LC	-	VR	?	V	-	P
272.	☐ **Tree Swallow**/Golodrina de Árboles/*Tachycineta bicolor*	LC	-	Co	-	WR-T	-	PC
273.	☐ **Bahama Swallow**/Golondrina de Bahamas/*Tachycineta cyaneoviridis*	LC	-	R	-	V	-	P
274.	☐ **Northern Rough-winged Swallow (Northern)**/Golodrina de Alas Ásperas/*Stelgidopteryx serripennis serripennis*	LC	-	FC	-	WR-T	-	PC
275.	☐ **Bank Swallow**/Golondrina de Collar/*Riparia riparia riparia*	LC	-	U	-	WR[77]-T	-	PC
276.	☐ **Cliff Swallow (pyrrhonota Group)**/Golondrina de Farallón/*Petrochelidon pyrrhonota pyrrhonota*	LC	-	R	-	T	-	P
277.	☐ **Cave Swallow (Caribbean)**/Golondrina de Cuevas/*Petrochelidon fulva cavicola*	LC	CU?	Co	Br	PM[s]	-	PC
278.	☐ **Barn Swallow (American)**/Golondrina Cola de Tijera/*Hirundo rustica erythrogaster*	LC	-	Co	-	WR[78]-T	-	PC

Order: PASSERIFORMES   Family: Troglodytidae

279.	☐ **Zapata Wren**/Ferminia/*Ferminia cerverai*	EN	CU	U	Br	YR	-	L
280.	☐ **House Wren (Northern)**/ Troglodita Americano/*Troglodytes aedon aedon*	LC	-	VR	-	V	-	P
281.	☐ **Marsh Wren**/Troglodita de Ciénaga/*Cistothorus palustris* (prob. *palustris*)	LC	-	VR	-	V	-	P

Order: PASSERIFORMES   Family: Polioptilidae

		Threat status	End. Reg.	Abun. status	Breed status	Resid. status	Int.	Dist.
282.	☐ Blue-gray Gnatcatcher/Rabudita/*Polioptila caerulea caerulea*	LC	-	Co	-	WR	-	PC
283.	☐ Cuban Gnatcatcher/Sinsontillo/*Polioptila lembeyei*	LC	CU	FC	Br	YR	-	R
	English Name/ Cuban Common Name (CCN)/ *Latin Name*	Threat status	End. Reg.	Abun. status	Breed status	Resid. status	Int.	Dist.
	Order: PASSERIFORMES Family: Regulidae							
284.	☐ Ruby-crowned Kinglet/Reyezuelo/*Regulus calendula calendula*	LC	-	R	-	V	-	P
	Order: PASSERIFORMES Family: Muscicapidae							
285.	☐ Northern Wheatear (Greenland)/Tordo del Ártico/*Oenanthe oenanthe leucorhoa*	LC	-	VR	-	V	-	P
	Order: PASSERIFORMES Family: Turdidae							
286.	☐ Eastern Bluebird (Eastern)/Azulejo Pechirrojo/*Sialia sialis sialis*	LC	-	R	-	WR-T	-	P
287.	☐ Cuban Solitaire/Ruiseñor/*Myadestes elisabeth elisabeth*	NT/VU	CU	FC	Br	YR	-	Rg
	☐ *Myadestes elisabeth retrusus*	Ex	CU	†	Br	YR	-	L
288.	☐ Veery/Tordo Colorado/*Catharus fuscescens fuscescens*	LC	-	U	-	T	-	P
	☐ *Catharus fuscescens salicicola*	LC	-	VR	-	T	-	P
289.	☐ Gray-cheeked Thrush/Tordo de Mejillas Grises/*Catharus minimus minimus*	LC	-	U	-	T	-	P
290.	☐ Bicknell's Thrush/Tordo de Bicknell/*Catharus bicknelli*	VU/EN	-	R	-	WR-T	-	L
291.	☐ Swainson's Thrush (Olive-backed)/Tordo de Espalda Olivada/*Catharus ustulatus swainsoni*[79]	LC	-	R	-	WR-T	-	P
292.	☐ Hermit Thrush/Tordo de Cola Colorada/*Catharus guttatus* (prob. *faxoni*)	LC	-	VR	-	V	-	P
293.	☐ Wood Thrush/Tordo Pecoso/*Hylocichla mustelina*	NT	-	R	-	WR-T	-	P
294.	☐ American Robin (migratorius Group)/Zorzal Migratorio/*Turdus migratorius migratorius*	LC	-	R	-	T	-	P
	☐ *Turdus migratorius achrusterus*	LC	-	VR	-	V	-	P
295.	☐ Red-legged Thrush (plumbeus/schistaceus)[80]/Zorzal Real/*Turdus plumbeus schistaceus*	LC	CU	Co	Br	YR	-	Rg
	☐ (rubripes/coryi)/*Turdus plumbeus rubripes*	LC	CU	Co	Br	YR	-	QC
	Order: PASSERIFORMES Family: Mimidae							
296.	☐ Gray Catbird/Zorzal Gato/*Dumetella carolinensis*	LC	-	Co	-	WR-T	-	PC
297.	☐ Brown Thrasher/Sinsonte Colorado/*Toxostoma rufum rufum*	LC	-	R	-	V	-	P
298.	☐ Bahama Mockingbird/Sinsonte Prieto/*Mimus gundlachii gundlachii*	LC/NT	GA-LY	U	Br	YR	-	L
299.	☐ Northern Mockingbird/Sinsonte/*Mimus polyglottos orpheus*	LC	-	Co	Br	YR	-	PC
	Order: PASSERIFORMES Family: Sturnidae							
300.	☐ European Starling/Estornino/*Sturnus vulgaris vulgaris*	LC	-	R	-	V	-	P
	Order: PASSERIFORMES Family: Bombycillidae							
301.	☐ Cedar Waxwing/Picotero del Cedro/*Bombycilla cedrorum cedrorum*	LC	-	U	-	WR-T	-	P
	Order: PASSERIFORMES Family: Estrildidae							
302.	☐ Scaly-breasted Munia (Checkered)/Damero/*Lonchura*	LC	-	FC	Br	YR	C1	PC

	English Name/ Cuban Common Name (CCN)/ *Latin Name*	Threat status	End. Reg.	Abun. status	Breed status	Resid. status	Int.	Dist.
	punctulata ssp.							
303.	☐ **Tricolored Munia**/Monjita Tricolor/*Lonchura malacca ssp.*[81]	LC	-	FC	Br	YR	C1	PC
304.	☐ **Chestnut Munia**/Monjita Castaña/*Lonchura atricapilla ssp.*[d]	LC	-	U	Br	YR	C1	L
	Order: PASSERIFORMES Family: Passeridae							
305.	☐ **House Sparrow**/Gorrión Doméstico/*Passer domesticus domesticus*	LC	-	Co	Br	YR	C1	PC
	Order: PASSERIFORMES Family: Motacillidae							
306.	☐ **American Pipit (rubescens/pacificus)**/Bisbita Norteamericana (SEO)/*Anthus rubescens rubescens*[82]	LC	-	R	-	V-WR?	-	P
	Order: PASSERIFORMES Family: Fringillidae							
307.	☐ **American Goldfinch**/Gorrión Amarillo/*Spinus tristis tristis*	LC	-	VR	-	V	-	P
	Order: PASSERIFORMES Family: Calcariidae							
308.	☐ **Lapland Longspur**/Escribano Lapón (SEO)/*Calcarius lapponicus lapponicus*[83]	LC	-	VR	-	V	-	P
	Order: PASSERIFORMES Family: Passerellidae							
309.	☐ **Green-tailed Towhee**/Gorrión de Cola Verde/*Pipilo chlorurus*	LC	-	VR	-	V	-	P
310.	☐ **Zapata Sparrow**/Cabrerito de la Ciénaga/*Torreornis inexpectata inexpectata*	EN	CU	U	Br	YR	-	L
	☐ *Torreornis inexpectata sigmani*	EN	CU	U	Br	YR	-	L
	☐ *Torreornis inexpectata varonai*	EN	CU	U	Br	YR	-	L
311.	☐ **Chipping Sparrow**/Gorrión de Cabeza Parda/*Spizella passerina passerina*	LC	-	R	-	V-WR?	-	P
312.	☐ **Clay-colored Sparrow**/Gorrión Colorado/*Spizella pallida*	LC	-	R	-	WR-T	-	P
313.	☐ **Lark Sparrow**/Gorrión de Uñas Largas /*Chondestes grammacus grammacus*	LC	-	R	-	V-T?	-	P
314.	☐ **Savannah Sparrow (Savannah)**/Gorrión de Sabana/*Passerculus sandwichensis sandwichensis*	LC	-	U	-	WR-T	-	QC
315.	☐ **Grasshopper Sparrow**/Chamberguito/*Ammodramus savannarum pratensis*	LC	-	U	-	WR-T	-	QC
316.	☐ **White-crowned Sparrow (*leucophrys*)**/Gorrión de Coronilla Blanca/*Zonotrichia leucophrys leucophrys*	LC	-	U	-	WR?-T	-	P
317.	☐ **Lincoln's Sparrow**/Gorrión de Lincoln/*Melospiza lincolnii lincolnii*	LC	-	R	-	WR-T	-	QC
318.	☐ **Dark-eyed Junco**/Junco de Ojos Oscuros/*Junco hyemalis* (prob. *hyemalis*)	LC	-	VR	-	V	-	P
	Order: PASSERIFORMES Family: Spindalidae							
319.	☐ **Western Spindalis** /Cabrero/*Spindalis zena pretrei*	LC	CU	Co	Br	YR	-	PC
	Order: PASSERIFORMES Family: Teretistridae							
320.	☐ **Yellow-headed Warbler**/ Chillina/*Teretistris fernandinae*[84]	LC	CU	Co	Br	YR	-	Rg
321.	☐ **Oriente Warbler** /Pechero/*Teretistris fornsi fornsi*[85]	LC	CU	Co	Br	YR	-	Rg
	☐ *Teretistris fornsi turquinensis*[86]	LC	CU	Co	Br	YR	-	L
	Order: PASSERIFORMES Family: Icteriidae							

#	English Name/ Cuban Common Name (CCN)/ *Latin Name*	Threat status	End. Reg.	Abun. status	Breed status	Resid. status	Int.	Dist.
322.	☐ **Yellow-breasted Chat (virens)**/Bijirita Grande/*Icteria virens virens*	LC	-	R	-	T	-	L

Order: PASSERIFORMES   Family: Icteridae

#	English Name/ Cuban Common Name (CCN)/ *Latin Name*	Threat status	End. Reg.	Abun. status	Breed status	Resid. status	Int.	Dist.
323.	☐ **Yellow-headed Blackbird**/Mayito de Cabeza Amarilla/*Xanthocephalus xanthocephalus*	LC	-	R	-	V	-	L
324.	☐ **Bobolink**/Chambergo/*Dolichonyx oryzivorus*	LC	-	FC	-	T	-	PC
325.	☐ **Eastern Meadowlark (Cuban)**/Sabanero/*Sturnella magna hyppocrepis*	LC	CU	Co	Br	YR	-	PC
326.	☐ **Cuban Oriole**/Solibio/*Icterus melanopsis*	LC	CU	Co	Br	YR	-	PC
327.	☐ **Orchard Oriole (Orchard)**/Turpial de Huertos/*Icterus spurius*	LC	-	U	-	T	-	P
328.	☐ **Hooded Oriole**/Turpial de Garganta Negra/*Icterus cucullatus* (prob. *igneus*)[87]	LC	-	XR	-	V	-	P
329.	☐ **Altamira Oriole**/Turpial de Altamira/*Icterus gularis ssp.* (prob. *mentalis*)	LC	-	XR	-	V	-	P
330.	☐ **Baltimore Oriole**/Turpial/*Icterus galbula*	LC	-	U	-	WR-T	-	PC
331.	☐ **Red-shouldered Blackbird**/Mayito de Ciénaga/*Agelaius assimilis assimilis*	VU	CU	FC	Br	YR	-	L
	☐ *Agelaius assimilis subniger*[88]	VU	CU	FC	Br	YR	-	L
332.	☐ **Tawny-shouldered Blackbird**/Mayito/*Agelaius humeralis scopulus*	LC	CU	FC	Br	YR	-	L
	☐ *Agelaius humeralis humeralis*	LC	GA	FC	Br	YR	-	PC
333.	☐ **Shiny Cowbird**/Pájaro Vaquero/*Molothrus bonariensis minimus*	LC	-	Co	Br	YR	-	PC
334.	☐ **Brown-headed Cowbird**/Totí Americano/*Molothrus ater ater*	LC	-	VR	-	V	-	P
335.	☐ **Cuban Blackbird**/Totí/*Ptiloxena atroviolacea*	LC	CU	Co	Br	YR	-	PC
336.	☐ **Greater Antillean Grackle**/Chichinguaco/*Quiscalus niger caribaeus*	LC	CU	Co	Br	YR	-	Rg
	☐ *Quiscalus niger gundlachii*	LC	CU	Co	Br	YR	-	QC

Order: PASSERIFORMES   Family: Parulidae

#	English Name/ Cuban Common Name (CCN)/ *Latin Name*	Threat status	End. Reg.	Abun. status	Breed status	Resid. status	Int.	Dist.
337.	☐ **Ovenbird**/Señorita de Monte/*Seiurus aurocapilla aurocapilla*	LC	-	Co	-	WR-T	-	PC
	☐ *Seiurus aurocapilla furvior*	LC	-	VR	-	V	-	P
338.	☐ **Worm-eating Warbler**/Bijirita Gusanera/*Helmitheros vermivorum*	LC	-	FC	-	WR-T	-	PC
339.	☐ **Louisiana Waterthrush**/Señorita de Río/*Parkesia motacilla*	LC	-	Co	-	WR-T	-	PC
340.	☐ **Northern Waterthrush**/Señorita de Manglar/*Parkesia noveboracensis noveboracensis*[89]	LC	-	Co	-	WR-T	-	PC
341.	☐ **Bachman's Warbler**/Bijirita de Bachman/*Vermivora bachmanii*	CR-Ex?	-	†?	-	WR	-	L
342.	☐ **Golden-winged Warbler**/Bijirita de Alas Doradas/*Vermivora chrysoptera*	NT	-	R	-	T	-	P
343.	☐ **Blue-winged Warbler**/Bijirita de Alas Azules/*Vermivora cyanoptera*	LC	-	R	-	WR-T	-	P
344.	☐ **Black-and-white Warbler**/Bijirita Trepadora/*Mniotilta varia*	LC	-	Co	-	WR-T	-	PC
345.	☐ **Prothonotary Warbler**/Bijirita Protonotaria/*Protonotaria citrea*	LC	-	FC	-	WR-T	-	PC
346.	☐ **Swainson's Warbler**/ Bijirita de Swainson/ *Limnothlypis swainsonii*	LC	-	U	-	WR-T	-	PC

	English Name/ Cuban Common Name (CCN)/ *Latin Name*	Threat status	End. Reg.	Abun. status	Breed status	Resid. status	Int.	Dist.
347.	☐ **Tennessee Warbler**/Bijirita de Tennessee/*Oreothlypis peregrina*[90]	LC	-	U	-	WR-T	-	PC
348.	☐ **Orange-crowned Warbler (celata)**/Bijirita de Coronilla Anaranjada/ *Oreothlypis celata celata*[91]	LC	-	R	-	V	-	P
349.	☐ **Nashville Warbler (ruficapilla)**/Bijirita de Nashville/*Oreothlypis ruficapilla ruficapilla*[92]	LC	-	R	-	V	-	P
350.	☐ **Virginia's Warbler**/Bijirita de Virginia/*Oreothlypis virginiae*[93]	LC	-	VR	-	V	-	P
351.	☐ **Mourning Warbler**/Bijirita de Cabeza Gris/*Geothlypis philadelphia*	LC	-	VR	-	V	-	P
352.	☐ **Kentucky Warbler**/Bijirita de Kentucky/*Geothlypis formosa*	LC	-	R	-	WR-T	-	P
353.	☐ **Common Yellowthroat (trichas Group)**/Caretica/*Geothlypis trichas trichas*	LC	-	Co	-	WR-T	-	PC
354.	☐ **Hooded Warbler**/Monjita/*Setophaga citrina*	LC	-	U	-	WR-T	-	PC
355.	☐ **American Redstart**/Candelita/*Setophaga ruticilla*	LC	-	Co	-[94]	WR[PM]	-	PC
356.	☐ **Kirtland´s Warbler**/Bijirita de Kirtland/*Setophaga kirtlandii*	NT	-	VR	-	V	-	P
357.	☐ **Cape May Warbler**/Bijirita Atigrada/*Setophaga tigrina*	LC	-	Co	-	WR-T	-	PC
358.	☐ **Cerulean Warbler**/Bijirita Azulosa/*Setophaga cerulea*	VU	-	R	-	T	-	P
359.	☐ **Northern Parula**/Bijirita Chica/*Setophaga americana*	LC	-	Co	-	WR-T	-	PC
360.	☐ **Magnolia Warbler**/Bijirita Magnolia/*Setophaga magnolia*	LC	-	Co	-	WR-T	-	PC
361.	☐ **Bay-breasted Warbler**/ Bijirita Castaña/*Setophaga castanea*	LC	-	R	-	T	-	QC
362.	☐ **Blackburnian Warbler**/Bijirita Blackburniana/*Setophaga fusca*	LC	-	R	-	T	-	P
363.	☐ **American Yellow Warbler (Northern)**/Canario de Manglar/*Setophaga petechia rubiginosa*	LC	-	R	-	T?	-	P
	☐ **(Northern)**/*Setophaga petechia aestiva*	LC	-	R	-	T	-	P
	☐ **(Golden)**/*Setophaga petechia gundlachi*	LC	-	Co	Br	YR	-	PC
364.	☐ **Chestnut-sided Warbler**/Bijirita de Costados Castaños/*Setophaga pensylvanica*	LC	-	U	-	T	-	QC
365.	☐ **Blackpoll Warbler**/Bijirita de Cabeza Negra/*Setophaga striata*	LC	-	FC	-	T	-	QC
366.	☐ **Black-throated Blue Warbler**/Bijirita Azul de Garganta Negra/ *Setophaga caerulescens caerulescens*	LC	-	Co	-	WR-T	-	PC
	☐ *Setophaga caerulescens cairnsi*	LC	-	R	-	WR	-	QC
367.	☐ **Palm Warbler (Western)**/Bijirita Común/*Setophaga palmarum palmarum*	LC	-	Co	-	WR-T	-	PC
	☐ **(Yellow)**/*Setophaga palmarum hypochrysea*[e]	LC	-	VR	-	WR?-T?	-	P
368.	☐ **Olive-capped Warbler**/Bijirita del Pinar/*Setophaga pityophila*[95]	LC/VU	CU-LY	Co	Br	YR	-	R
369.	☐ **Pine Warbler**/Bijirita de Pinos/*Setophaga pinus pinus*	LC	-	R	-	WR-T	-	P
370.	☐ **Yellow-rumped Warbler (Myrtle)**/Bijirita Coronada/*Setophaga coronata coronata*	LC	-	FC	-	WR-T	-	PC
	☐ **(Audubon´s)**/*Setophaga coronata auduboni* [f, 96]	LC	-	VR	-	V	-	P
371.	☐ **Yellow-throated Warbler (dominica/stoddardi)**/Bijirita de Garganta Amarilla/*Setophaga dominica dominica*[97]	LC	-	Co	-	WR-T	-	PC
	☐ **(dominica/stoddardi)**/*Setophaga dominica stoddardi*	LC	-	R	-	WR-T	-	PC
	☐ **(albilora)**/*Setophaga dominica albilora*	LC	-	U	-	WR-T	-	P

		Threat status	End. Reg.	Abun. status	Breed status	Resid. status	Int.	Dist.
372.	☐ **Prairie Warbler**/Mariposa Galana/*Setophaga discolor discolor*	LC	-	Co	-	WR-T	-	PC
	☐ *Setophaga discolor paludicola*	LC	-	Co	-	WR-T	-	PC
	English Name/ Cuban Common Name (CCN)/ *Latin Name*	Threat status	End. Reg.	Abun. status	Breed status	Resid. status	Int.	Dist.
373.	☐ **Black-throated Gray Warbler**/Bijirita Gris/*Setophaga nigrescens ssp.*[98]	LC	-	VR	-	V	-	P
374.	☐ **Townsend's Warbler**/Bijirita de Townsend/*Setophaga townsendi*	LC	-	VR	-	V	-	P
375.	☐ **Black-throated Green Warbler**/Bijirita de Garganta Negra/*Setophaga virens*	LC	-	Co	-	WR-T	-	PC
376.	☐ **Canada Warbler**/Bijirita de Canadá/*Cardellina canadensis*[99]	LC	-	VR	-	T	-	P
377.	☐ **Wilson's Warbler (pileolata)**/Bijirita de Wilson/ *Cardellina pusilla pileolata*[g]	LC	-	VR	-	T	-	P
	☐ **(pusilla)**/*Cardellina pusilla pusilla*	LC	-	R	-	T	-	P
	Order: PASSERIFORMES Family: Cardinalidae							
378.	☐ **Summer Tanager**/Cardenal Rojo/*Piranga rubra rubra*	LC	-	FC	-	WR-T	-	QC
379.	☐ **Scarlet Tanager**/Cardenal Alinegro/*Piranga olivacea*	LC	-	U	-	WR?-T	-	PC
380.	☐ **Western Tanager**/Cardenal del Oeste/*Piranga ludoviciana*	LC	-	VR	-	V	-	P
381.	☐ **Rose-breasted Grosbeak**/Degollado/*Pheucticus ludovicianus*	LC	-	FC	-	WR-T	-	PC
382.	☐ **Blue Grosbeak**/Azulejón/*Passerina caerulea caerulea*	LC	-	FC	-	WR-T	-	PC
383.	☐ **Lazuli Bunting**/Mariposa Azul/*Passerina amoena*	LC	-	VR	-	V	-	P
384.	☐ **Indigo Bunting**/Azulejo/*Passerina cyanea*	LC	-	FC	-[100]	WR-T	-	PC
385.	☐ **Painted Bunting**/Mariposa/*Passerina ciris ciris*	NT/ VU	-	U	-	WR-T	-	PC
386.	☐ **Dickcissel**/Gorrión de Pecho Amarillo/*Spiza americana*	LC	-	R	-	T	-	PC
	Order: PASSERIFORMES Family: Thraupidae							
387.	☐ **Saffron Finch**/Gorrión Azafrán/*Sicalis flaveola ssp.*[101]	LC	-	VR	-	V	C5?	P
388.	☐ **Blue-black Grassquit**/Arrocero Negrito/*Volatinia jacarina splendens*[102]	LC	-	XR	-	V	?	P
389.	☐ **Red-legged Honeycreeper**/Aparecido de San Diego/*Cyanerpes cyaneus carneipes*	LC	-	Co	Br	YR	?	PC
390.	☐ **Bananaquit (Bahamas)**/Reinita/*Coereba flaveola bahamensis*	LC	-	R	-	V- YR?	-	P
391.	☐ **Cuban Grassquit**/Tomeguín del Pinar/*Tiaris canorus*[103]	LC	CU	FC	Br	YR	-	PC
392.	☐ **Yellow-faced Grassquit**/Tomeguín de la Tierra/*Tiaris olivaceus olivaceus*	LC	-	Co	Br	YR	-	PC
393.	☐ **Black-faced Grassquit**/Tomeguín Prieto/*Tiaris bicolor bicolor*[104]	LC	-	R	Br	PM	-	P
394.	☐ **Cuban Bullfinch**/Negrito/*Melopyrrha nigra*[105]	LC/ NT	CU	FC	Br	YR	-	PC

Hypothetical Forms

Species that have been mentioned in different media but with doubtful, uncertain or unsatisfactory confirmation status for the Cuban archipelago (see General Comments).

	English Name/ Cuban Common Name (CCN)/ *Latin Name*
	Order: ANSERIFORMES Family: Anatidae
1.	☐ **Greater Scaup**/Pato Cabezón Raro/*Aythya marila neartica*[106]
2.	☐ **Common Goldeneye**/Porrón Osculado (SEO)/*Bucephala clangula*[107]
	Order: APODIFORMES Family: Apodidae
3.	☐ **Black Swift (borealis)**/Vencejo Negro/*Cypseloides niger borealis*[108]
	Order: PASSERIFORMES Family: Corvidae
4.	☐ **Blue Jay**/Chara Azul (SEO)/*Cyanocitta cristata*[109]
	Order: PASSERIFORMES Family: Fringillidae
5.	☐ **Pine Siskin**/Jilguero de los Pinos (SEO)/*Spinus pinus*[110]
	Order: PASSERIFORMES Family: Parulidae
6.	☐ **Connecticut Warbler**/Bijirita de Connecticut/*Oporornis agilis*[111]
	Order: PASSERIFORMES Family: Icteridae
7.	☐ **Yellow-tailed Oriole**/Turpial de Cola Amarilla/*Icterus mesomelas*[112] *ssp.*
8.	☐ **Rusty Blackbird**/Zanate Canadiense (SEO)/*Euphagus carolinus ssp.*[113]
	Order: PASSERIFORMES Family: Cardinalidae
9.	☐ **Northern Cardinal**/Cardenal Norteño (SEO) /*Cardinalis cardinalis ssp.*[114]
10.	☐ **Painted Bunting**/Mariposa/*Passerina ciris pallidior*[115]
	Order: PASSERIFORMES Family: Ploceidae
11.	☐ **Bold Village Weaver**/Tejedor Común (SEO) /*Ploceus cucullatus*[116]

Other exotics, introduced and uncertain origin species

Species recorded as introductions, human-assisted transportees or escapees from captivity, and whose breeding populations (if any) are thought not to be self-sustaining. These birds should not be considered part of the Cuban avifauna and are not included in the main list.

	English Name/ Cuban Common Name (CCN)/ *Latin Name*	Category
	Order: Tinamiformes Family: Tinamidae	
1.	☐ **Tinamou**/Tinamidae sp. (not specified)[117]	C6
	Order: GALLIFORMES Family: Cracidae	
2.	☐ **Plain Chachalaca**/Chachalaca norteña/*Ortalis vetula ssp.*[118]	C6

	English Name/ Cuban Common Name (CCN)/ *Latin Name*	Category
	Order: GALLIFORMES Family: Odontophoridae	
3.	☐ **California Quail**/Colín de Clifornia (SEO)/*Callipepla californica ssp.*[118]	C6
4.	☐ **Montezuma Quail**/Colín de Montezuma/*Cyrtonyx montezumae ssp.*[118]	C6
	Order: GALLIFORMES Family: Phasianidae	
5.	☐ **Barbary Partridge**/Perdiz Moruna (SEO)/*Alectoris barbara ssp.*[118]	C6
6.	☐ **Ocelated Turkey**/Guajolote (Pavo) Ocelado/*Meleagris ocellata*[119]	C6
	Order: GRUIFORMES Family: Rallidae	
7.	☐ **Wood Rail (not specified)**/Cotara (SEO) Gallinuela (sin especificar)/*Aramides sp.*[120]	C6
	Order: CHARADRIIFORMES Family: Burhinidae	
8.	☐ **Thick-knee (not specified)**/Alcaraván (sin especificar)/*Burhinus sp.*[121]	C6
	Order: CORACIIFORMES Family: Alcedinidae	
9.	☐ **Common Kingfisher (Common)**/Martín Pescador Europeo/*Alcedo atthis ssp.*[122]	E?
	Order: PSITTACIFORMES Family: Psittacidae	
10.	☐ **Cockatiel**/Cacatillo/*Nymphicus holandicus*	E
11.	☐ **Budgerigar**/Periquito de Australia/*Melopsittacus undulatus*	E
	Order: PSITTACIFORMES Family: Psittaculidae	
12.	☐ **Rose-ringed Parakeet**/Periquito Rosado (SEO)/*Psittacula krameri ssp.*	E
13.	☐ **Rossy-faced Lovebird**/Agapornis/*Agapornis roseicolis ssp.*[123]	E
	Order: PASSERIFORMES Family: Corvidae	
14.	☐ **House Crow**/Cuervo de la India/*Corvus splendens ssp.*[124]	E
	Order: PASSERIFORMES Family: Pygnonotidae	
15.	☐ **White-eared Bubul**/Bulbul Cariblanco (SEO)/*Pycnonotus leucotis ssp.*	E (C5?)
	Order: PASSERIFORMES Family: Silviidae	
16.	☐ **Eurasian Blackcap**/Curruca Capirotada (SEO)/*Sylvia atricapilla ssp.*[125]	E?
	Order: PASSERIFORMES Family: Timaliidae	
17.	☐ **Scarlet-faced Liocichla**/Charlatán de Rippon (SEO)/*Liocichla ripponi*[126]	E
18.	☐ **Red-billed Leiothrix**/Leiothrix Piquirrojo (SEO)/*Leiothrix lutea ssp.*	E

	English Name/ Cuban Common Name (CCN)/ *Latin Name*	Category
	Order: PASSERIFORMES Family: Sturnidae	
19.	☐ **Crested Myna**/Miná Crestado/*Acridotheres cristatellus ssp.*[127]	E?
	Order: PASSERIFORMES Family: Passerellidae	
20.	☐ **Rufous-collared Sparrow**/Chingolo Común (SEO)/*Zonotricia capensis ssp.*[128]	E?
	Order: PASSERIFORMES Family: Fringillidae	
21.	☐ **European Goldfinch**/Jilguero/*Carduelis carduelis ssp.*[129]	C6?
22.	☐ **Lesser Goldfinch**/Chichí Bacal/*Spinus psaltria jouyi*[130]	C6
23.	☐ **Red Siskin**/Jilguero Rojo/*Spinus cucullatus*[131]	E?
24.	☐ **Island Canary (Domestic Type)**/Canario/*Serinus canaria*	E
	Order: PASSERIFORMES Family: Thraupidae	
25.	☐ **Red-crested Cardinal**/Cardellina crestada/*Paroaria coronata*[132]	E
26.	☐ **Red-cowled Cardinal**/Cardellina dominica (SEO)/*Paroaria dominicana*[133]	E
27.	☐ **Cinnamon-rumped Seedeater**/Semillero Torcaz (SEO)/*Sporophila torqueola*[134]	E?
	Order: PASSERIFORMES Family: Passeridae	
28.	☐ **Sudan Golden Sparrow**/Gorrión Dorado/*Passer luteus*[135]	E?
29.	☐ **White-winged Snowfinch**/Gorrión Alpino (SEO)/*Montifringilla nivalis ssp.*	E?
	Order: PASSERIFORMES Family: Ploceidae	
30.	☐ **Bishop sp.**/Obispo sp./*Euplectes cf. hordaceus/afer*[136]	C5?/E ?
31.	☐ **Yellow-mantled Widowbird**/Obispo Cornigualdo (SEO)/*Euplectes macroura macroura*[137]	E
	Order: PASSERIFORMES Family: Estrildidae	
32.	☐ **Gouldian Finch**/Lady Gould/*Chloebia gouldiae* (domestic)	E
33.	☐ **Java Sparrow**/Gorrión de Java/*Lonchura orizivora*	E

GENERAL COMMENTS

New additions

References supporting the new forms recorded on the Cuban archipelago November 2017-2018.

As a point of reference, notes are based on species recorded in Garrido and García, (1975) and Garrido and Kirkconnell, (2011). New additions will be updated every year at the species and subspecies levels. I gave priority in eBird to the sightings of a rare bird that has photos or any other media where the bird has been clearly identified. (sp) Species level; (ssp) Subspecific level.

a (ssp) **King Rail (Northern) (*Rallus elegans elegans*):** Recorded by Garrido, 1988.

b (sp) **Curlew Sandpiper (*Calidirs ferruginea*):** Registered on two occasions in groups between 65 and 85 birds in the South Pinar del Río wetlands between Los Palacios and Consolación del Sur municipalities (Castro *et al.*, 2018 *in press.*), birds show winter and molting plumages (Rodolfo Castro, 2018 com pers.).

c (sp) **Caribbean Martin (*Progne dominicensis*):** The bird was identified by the author from a picture taken by Moth Clark in Playa Esmeralda, Hotel Río de Luna y Mares, Rafael Freyre, Holguín province. Subsequently the sighting was uploaded to eBird by the author of this paper; it corresponds to the first record of this species for Cuba. https://ebird.org/view/checklist/S44988022. Supported by a photo of an adult male where field marks are clear, in particular, the white vent patch and black breast.

d (sp) **Chestnut Munia (*Lonchura atricapilla*):** Amended. Apparently these sightings resulted from *lapsus calami* by Garrido and Wiley (2010). They mentioned Chestnut Mannikin (Munia), a name also used to refer to Tricolored Mannikin (Munia) (*L. malacca*). At this time the form *atricapilla* was considered conspecific to *malacca* (at the time Chestnut) now considered a full species, and later mentioned in Rodríguez *et al.* (2017), referring to the former paper but using the current Latin name (*L. atricapilla*) for Chestnut Munia. I could not find any publication that placed *atricapilla sensu stricto* in Cuba. I did find a small private "zoo" owned by Carlos Cuadrado, who is also a local bird trapper in Gibara (Holguín Province). In 2013, Cuadrado caught several individuals in Viola, 10 km south of Gibara. I was able to closely examine the birds together with Tricolored Munias (*L. malacca*). Cuadrado also mentioned a local population that breeds in the area, where it was locally common. I did not realize the importance of this sighting at the time as they were treated as conspecific. Recently my friend Feliberto Bermúdez, an avid local naturalist with extensive experience with birds, found that flocks are still around, especially between Calderón and La Presa, in the surrounding areas of Viola, Gibara. This mention is the first official record for the Chestnut Munia (*L. atricapilla*) in Cuba.

e (ssp) **Palm Warbler (Yellow) (*Setophaga palmarum hypochrysea*): eBird.** Christopher Rustay. A-1 Gas Station, Villa Clara, 2012. ebird.org/view/checklist/S12250172. No photos available but field notes with good and complete descriptions of the sighting.

f (ssp) **Yellow-rumped Warbler (Audubon´s) (*Setophaga coronata auduboni*): eBird.** Observed by the author accompanied by Maikel Cañizares Morera and Aslam Ibraim Castellón Maure during an expedition to Cabo de San Antonio. Supported by photos of a bird in fall plumage showing yellow on the throat and lacking the white superciliary stripe. ebird.org/caribbean/view/checklist/S40652229.

g (ssp) **Wilson's Warbler (pileolata) (*Cardellina pusilla pileolata*):** Record published in "Nuevos registros de aves para la península de Guanahacabibes, que incluyen el primer registro de *Cardellina pusilla pileolata* para Cuba." (Llanes *et al.*, 2016).

Comments

[1] **Black-bellied Whistling-Duck (fulgens)** (*Dendrocygna autumnalis fulgens*): Origin of type specimen unclear, leading to confusion over correct allocation of nominate subspecies *Dendrocygna autumnalis autumnalis*; S race has been labelled *discolor*, with N race then as nominate, but re-examination of the literature indicates that *autumnalis* should be applied to S population, with N population then named *fulgens*. Northern race is distinctive, lacking grey lower breast to hindcollar, but other differences apparently minor. Races intergrade in Panama (Carboneras and Kirwan, 2018).

Photographs taken by local hunters in Cuba resulted in the northern form *fulgens*. The sample from Holguín Museum of Natural History assigned by Garrido and García (1975) to the former race *discolor* (now *autumnalis*) appears to be intermediate, but it clearly matched the northern form also. This sample had been exposed to daylight for a long time and some color faded. Confusion could be generated because of a rare color pattern where the medium belly remains grayish, perhaps pertaining to an immature of a rare color pattern of *fulgens*. In any case the cinnamon color on this sample extends onto the back, matching the *fulgens* populations, while in *autumnalis* (the southern subspecies) the grey extends onto the back. Garrido and García (1975) also reported introductions in Cuba in 1931, but the bird also occurs by natural means.

[2] **Fulvous Whistling-Duck** (*Dendrocygna bicolor*): Status change to Partial Migrant (PM), previously considered as Year Round (YR). Blanco and Sanchez, 2005 found recovered rings from birds banded in North America.

[3] **Blue-winged Teal** (*Spatula discors*): Breeding and Resident status changes, formerly considered a Winter Resident (WR) and Transient (T), further surveys found that Year Round (YR) populations remain in western Cuba (Castro, *et al*, *in press*); same condition has been found in St. Croix, Virgin Islands (Yntena, *et al*., 2017). Logically it could be considered a Partial Migrant (PM). Unpublished data suggest the possibility of breeding (Rodolfo Castro *com. pers.*, 2018).

[4] **White-winged Scoter (North American)** (*Melanitta fusca deglandi*): Taxa *deglandi* and *stejnegeri*, previously included in present species (*fusca*), have sometimes been separated and treated as a single species (*M. deglandi*) by some principal international lists, following Collinson M. *et al.* (2006), remaining *fusca* to refer to the monotypic old-world populations called Velvet Scoter. The main distinguishing features are the shape and colour of the bill, the size of the white eye-patch and the colour of the flanks.

[5] **Northern Bobwhite (Eastern)** (*Colinus virginianus cubanensis*): Treated here as a Cuban endemic subspecies. Gundlach (1873) and Bond (1948) proposed that Bobwhite populations in Cuba were the result of an introduction by European settlers, whereas Ridgway (1894) argued that two distinct Bobwhite populations existed in Cuba: native populations representing *cubanensis* and introduced birds from Florida (*floridanus*). Cuban bobwhite populations represent a conundrum with regard to the geographic range of the Northern Bobwhite. Recent molecular studies could not find unique haplotypes for Cuban populations suggesting that the colonization of the island by Bobwhites is recent, most likely the result of introductions by European colonists. We cannot reject the possibility that Florida Bobwhites (*C. v. floridanus*) were introduced to Cuba during the late 1800s and early 1900s, and may have "genetically swamped" an older, native Bobwhite population. However, it seems as plausible that Bobwhites sampled in Cuba descended from introductions from Mexico and the United States by European settlers (Williford, 2013). D'Orbigny (1837-1861) also mentioned this species (*Ortyx virginianus*) saying that it was particularly common in Cuba at this time.

[6] **Plain Pigeon** (*Patagioenas inornata inornata*): Some lists do not accept any of the currently described races as valid: *wetmorei* is said to be deeper in colour, with white edging on wings broader on average; and *exigua* is reported to be even deeper in colour, with a white eye surrounded by red orbital skin (Baptista *et al.*, 2018).

[7] **Eurasian Collared-Dove** (*Streptopelia decaocto decaocto*): Sometimes treated as conspecific with *S. roseogrisea* but differs vocally and genetically, and also in plumage and biometrics. Considered Monotypic. Race *xanthocycla* had been hitherto considered conspecific with *S. decaocto*, but has darker grey on head, with forehead grey not whitish-grey; underparts more strongly tinged pinkish and slightly darker; broad yellow eyering; longer tail, which results in outertail feathers showing equivalently more white; slightly different song, with same rhythm and structure of three-note strophe, but pitch higher at start and each note lower than the last, creating a greater cadence, for this reason, sometimes split as a full species. Proposed race *stoliczkae* of Chinese Turkestan based on feral birds (del Hoyo, *et al.* 2018).

[8] **Great Lizard-Cuckoo (Cuban)** (*Coccyzus merlini*): Considered by some authors as a full species. Bahamas population has been separated as a full species (*C. bahamensis*) by the absence of rufous wingpanel, since outer vanes of primaries are concolorous with wing and all upperparts, although inner vanes are rufous and show up in flight; black tip of uppertail; and (by comparison with *decolor* from Isle of Youth, which most

closely resembles *bahamensis* in lacking rufous tone to upperparts) purer grey on breast and paler rufous on lower underparts. (Payne *et al.*, 2018). I don´t recognize this treatment as valid; the characteristics used for separation of both forms are weak, also there is an absence of a published taxonomic arrangement comparing both populations.

[9] **Antillean Nighthawk** (*Chordeiles gundlachii gundlachii*): Sometimes considered monotypic. Northern populations (Florida and Bahamas) separated as race *vicinus*, supposedly smaller and lacking tawny morph (Cleere and Kirwan, 2018).

[10] **Northern Potoo (Caribbean)** (*Nyctibius jamaicensis ssp.*): Two birds have been collected, a female and a male respectively; the first sample was a skin (probably a female) identified for the first time by me in the Holguín Museum of Natural History (MNHNH). Later I advised Arturo Kirkconnell and we visited the area, but failed to find new evidence. A few weeks later another individual, probably a male (now in the MNHNH) was collected by the local people in the same place, Santa Cruz, a small village located about 18 km south of the city of Holguin, in a secondary forest near the city garbage dump. Other sightings based on observations were published previously by Martinez *et al.*, 2000 and Kirwan, 2001. The birds are closer to the nominate subspecies from Jamaica and quite different from the Hispaniolan (*abboti*), which has an overall greyish coloration. The Cuban birds are browner and darker than Jamaican populations; while similar, further studies are needed to clarify the status of the Cuban populations.

[11] **Order: APODIFORMES Family: Apodidae**: Some authors include Potoos, Swifts and Hummingbirds in Caprimulgiformes.

[12] **Order: APODIFORMES Family: Trochilidae**: Some authors include Hummingbirds in Caprimulgiformes.

[13] **Bahama Woodstar** (*Calliphlox evelynae*): Currently, populations have been split and are considered two full species in Chesser *et al.* 2015: *C. evelynae* (Bahamas and Caicos) and *C. lyrura* (restricted to Inagua). There is no detailed description in Kirkconnell and Kirwan, 2008 to clarify to which taxa the individual pertained. Other principal international lists still treat both as conspecific (Schuchmann *et al.*, 2018).

[14] **Cuban Emerald** (*Chlorostilbon ricordii*): At times Cuban and Bahamian populations have been treated as different subspecies; currently this has been rejected by nearly all the principal international bird lists.

[15] **Zapata Rail** (*Cyanolimnas cerverai*): The last surveys (Navarro, *et al.* 2016-2017 Pamela and Alexander Skutch Progress Report) in Zapata Swamp failed to obtain any graphic demonstration of the bird´s existence. Navarro (Pamela and Alexander Skutch Award Progress report) found that the last official graphic reference of the species was a B/W photograph taken by Pedro Ragalado in February, 1971, in the area of Santo Tomás, the Type Locality of this species. New surveys need to be undertaken; the Swamp has been completely flooded for over a year because of heavy rains and hurricanes. The lack of logistic availability such as the large bureaucratic process and local government regulations involved for the use of boats (to allow movement within the swamp) are the main obstacles to undertaking extended surveys in the core zone. Previous expeditions have been focused mainly in the peripheral areas, which are prone to be affected by anthropic causes like fires.

[16] **Spotted Rail** (*Pardirallus maculatus maculatus*): Possible race *inoptatus* (W Cuba) included in nominate because of the lack of diagnostic characteristics, which overlap with those from the nominate race (Watson, 1962).

[17] **American Coot** (*Fulica americana*): *Fulica caribaea* has been merged into this species based on evidence of non-assortative mating and lack of diagnosable morphological differences (Chesser *et al.*, 2016).

[18] **American Avocet** (*Recurvirostra Americana*): Status change to Breeding (Br). Labrada and Blanco, 2011 found a breeding colony in Birama Swamp, eastern Cuba.

[19] **American Oystercatcher** (*Haematopus palliatus palliatus*): Hernández, 2006 reported the first breeding records for the species in Cuba in Cayuelo del Mono, north of Villa Clara Province.

[20] **Black-bellied Plover** (*Pluvialis squatarola squatarola*): Status change to Partial Migrant (PM), previously considered as Winter Resident (WR) and Transient (T). eBird, 2018 sightings show that birds remain in Cuba year round. No breeding records have been found; further studies required.

[21] **Snowy Plover (nivosus)** (*Charadrius nivosus nivosus*): Status change to Partial Migrant (PM), previously

considered as Year Round (YR). Blanco and Sanchez, 2011 suggested modifying the status based on fluctuations in frequency and abundance in local populations and sightings where birds had metal rings, suggesting they were banded in North America or, at least, not in Cuba; no Snowy Plover has been banded in Cuba.

[22] **Wilson's Plover** (*Charadrius wilsonia wilsonia*): Status change to Partial Migrant (PM), previously considered a Summer Resident (SR). Blanco and Sanchez, 2011 found fluctuation in the year round abundance suggesting migrant birds could increase the number of birds in the population.

[23] **Whimbrel (Hudsonian)** (*Numenius phaeopus hudsonicus*): Recently given species rank by one authority on the basis of "diagnostic differences in plumage and mean morphometric differences" plus mtDNA divergence of 3.6%, but it is not currently recognized because of the lack of enough diagnosable characteristics (Van Gils *et al.*, 2018).

[24] **Ruddy Turnstone** (*Arenaria interpres morinella*): Resident status changes. It was considered a Winter Resident (WR) and Transient (T) for Cuba. eBird evidence (supported by photos) shows that some birds remain in Cuba Year Round (YR), (eBird, 2018). Non-breeding birds have been found; further studies are needed.

[25] **Red Knot** (*Calidris canutus ssp.*): Status change to Winter Resident-Transient (WR-T) following Blanco, 2006; see also eBird 2018. Previously considered Transient (T).

[26] **Sanderling** (*Calidris alba*): Often treated as monotypic, but separation of race *rubida* appears to be justifiable. There are few genetic differences, however, between birds from NE Greenland and C Siberia. Two subspecies recognized in other international lists (Van Gils *et al.*, 2018).

[27] **Greater Yellowlegs** (*Tringa melanoleuca*): Considered a Winter Resident (WR) and Transient (T) for Cuba. eBird evidence (unsupported by photos) suggests that some birds remain in Cuba Year Round (YR), (eBird, 2018). These sightings are not substantial enough to modify its status yet; further data is needed.

[28] **Lesser Yellowlegs**/*Tringa flavipes*: Considered a Winter Resident (WR) and Transient (T) for Cuba. eBirds evidence (unsupported by photos) suggests that some birds remain in Cuba Year Round (YR), (eBird, 2018). These sightings are not substantial enough to modify its status yet; further data is needed.

[29] **Willet (Western)** (*Tringa semipalmata inornata*): Two subspecies recognized. Genetic, but also morphological, ecological, and behavioral differences suggest that the two subspecies may merit treatment as separate species (Oswald *et al.* 2016).

[30] **Wilson's Phalarope** (*Phalaropus tricolor*): Sometimes subsumed into *Steganopus*, results suggest that it is genetically distinct from *Phalaropus*, and with several ecological and morphological differences. Possibly quite close to *Tringa* (Van Gils *et al.*, 2018). The proposal to resurrect the genus *Steganopus* was rejected by Chesser et al, 2017.

[31] **Bonaparte's Gull** (*Chroicocephalus philadelphia*): Status of Transient (T) added, following Blanco and Sanchez, 2011, previously considered Winter Resident (WR).

[32] **Herring Gull (American)** (*Larus argentatus smithsonianus*): Race *smithsonianus* sometimes treated as a full species (HBW Alive). Morphologically, however, it is so slightly divergent that adults are "near-indistinguishable" from *argentatus*; moreover, acceptance of the split comes with the caveat that "splits or lumps based *solely* on mtDNA cannot be regarded as robust" (del Hoyo *et al.*, 2018).

[33] **Brown Noddy** (*Anous stolidus stolidus*): Status of Transient (T) added, following Blanco and Sanchez, 2011. Previously considered just Summer Resident (SR).

[34] **Bridled Tern** (*Onychoprion anaethetus recognitus*): Geographical variation subtle and subspecific divisions probably exaggerated; taxonomy in need of revision. Proposed form *recognitus* (from West Indies, Belize and islands off N Venezuela) is included in *melanopterus* (Gochfeld, *et al.*, 2018).

[35] **Least Tern** (*Sternula antillarum antillarum*): Status change to Partial Migrant (PM) following Blanco and Sanchez, 2011, see also eBird 2018; previously considered a Summer Resident (SR)-Transient (T).

[36] **Gull-billed Tern (Gull-billed)**/*Gelochelidon nilotica aranea*: Status change to Partial Migrant (PM), following

Blanco and Sanchez, 2011). Previously treated as Winter Resident (WR) and Transient (T).

[37] **Caspian Tern** (*Hydroprogne caspia*): Considered a Winter Resident (WR) and Transient (T) for Cuba. eBird evidence (supported by photos) suggests that some birds remain in Cuba Year Round (YR), (eBird, 2018), and Castro *et al.*, 2018 (*in press*). Between two and six individuals per month from May to September have been seen resting and feeding in the south Pinar del Río wetlands.

[38] **Roseate Tern** (*Sterna dougallii dougallii*): Status change to Partial Migrant (PM) following Blanco and Sanchez, 2011; previously considered a Summer Resident (SR) and Transient (T). The breeding status was missed in the previous Annotated Checklist (Navarro and Reyes, 2017).

[39] **Common Tern (hirundo)** (*Sterna hirundo hirundo*): Status change to Partial Migrant (PM) following Blanco and Sanchez, 2011, previously considered a Transient (T).

[40] **Sandwich Tern (Cayenne)** (*Thalasseus sandvicensis eurygnatus*): Other lists consider just two subspecies (*sandvicensis* and *acuflavidus*). Recent genetic studies suggest the race *acuflavidus* may be closer to *T. elegans* than *sandvicensis*; juveniles of the two are highly divergent, but becoming increasingly alike with age. Form *eurygnathus* ("Cayenne Tern"; often misspelt *eurygnatha*) previously considered a separate species, but S Caribbean data indicate it is a race or perhaps morph of *T. sandvicensis*, and that all New World populations (except those of extreme N) have at least a small percentage of "Cayenne"-type birds; based on recent genetic studies. This is why *eurygnathus* is sometimes treated as a synonym of *acuflavidus*; the two interbreed freely in S Caribbean (Gochfeld, *et al.*, 2018). The first record of this form was made in 2005 in Cayo Felipe de Barlovento in the northern Ciego de Ávila province (Pérez *et al.*, 2005).

[41] **Family: Oceanitidae**: Chesser, *et al.*, 2018 recognized a new family Oceanitidae and moved the genera Oceanites, Pelagodroma, and Fregetta to this family as indicated by the text of this supplement.

[42] **Leach's Storm-Petrel (Leach´s)** (*Oceanodroma leucorhoa*): Sometimes incorporates *Oceanodroma*, within which *Hydrobates* was found in recent studies to be embedded; since *Hydrobates* is the older name, it is used for this expanded genus (Carboneras, *et al.*, 2018).

[43] **Band-rumped Storm-Petrel** (*Oceanodroma castro*): *Idem*.

[44] **Cory's Shearwater (borealis)** (*Calonectris diomedea borealis*): Sometimes treated as a full species, molecular evidence supports this split in one study, but is equivocal in another, with further research needed. (del Hoyo *et al.*, 2018).

[45] **Audubon's Shearwater** (*Puffinus iherminieri iherminieri*): The first breeding record of the species was done in Cayo Felipe de Barlovento, a small key in the north of Ciego de Avila province (Rodríguez *et al.*, 2008).

[46] **Magnificent Frigatebird** (*Fregata magnificens*): Sometimes considered polytypic (HBW Alive), considering three subspecies. Race *rothschildi*, which supposedly inhabits the area, has commonly not been accepted. Further studies are required (Orta *et al.*, 2018).

[47] **American White Pelican** (*Pelecanus erythrorhynchos*): Breeding and Resident status changes, formerly considered a Winter Resident (WR) and Transient (T), further surveys found Year Round (YR) populations remain in western Cuba (Castro, *et al*, *in press*) during subsequent years. There are also sightings from eBird in other places (eBird, 2018). For this reason I decided to change the status to Partial Migrant (PM).

[48] **American Bittern** (*Botaurus lentiginosus*): Considered a Winter Resident (WR) and Transient (T) for Cuba. eBird evidence (unsupported by photos) suggests that some birds could remain in Cuba Year Round (YR), (eBird, 2018). These sightings are not substantial enough to modify its status yet; further data is needed.

[49] **Great Blue Heron** (*Ardea herodias occidentalis*): Race *occidentalis*, mostly white-morph birds, previously considered a distinct species. Possible hybrid *occidentalis* × *wardi* with white head, described as different species, Würdemann's Heron (*A. wurdemanni*); recent opinion suggests that it is merely a colour morph of *wardi* or *occidentalis* (Martínez-Vilalta *et al.* (a), 2018).

[50] **Green Heron (virescens/bahamensis)** (*Butorides virescens virescens*): Sometimes considered conspecific with *B. striata* (Martínez-Vilalta *et al.* (b), 2018).

[51] **White Ibis** (*Eudocimus albus*): Status change to Partial Migrant (PM), previously considered Year Round

(YR), birds banded in North America have been recovered in Cuba (Dennis and Salvat, 2006). Closely related to *E. ruber*. Proposal to merge the two into a single species on the basis of close morphological and ecological similarities and natural hybridization in zone of overlap in Venezuela (where more than 40 mixed pairs were recorded); another view is that they may simply be colour morphs. Here, the case for lumping considered not proven. Two subspecies are sometimes recognized (*albus* and *ramobustorum*) (Mathew et al., 2018).

[52] **Scarlet Ibis** (*Eudocimus ruber*): Closely related to *E. albus*. Proposal to merge the two into a single species on the basis of close morphological and ecological similarities and natural hybridization in zone of overlap in Venezuela. (Mathew *et al.*, 2018). Even though there are more than two visual records for Cuba (Acosta and Torres, 1996) I decided to consider keeping it as Very Rare until new official publications are available.

[53] **Glossy Ibis** (*Plegadis falcinellus*): Closely related to *P. chihi*, which was formerly considered a race of present species; hybrids reported in captivity, but not known under natural conditions in narrow zone of overlap (S Louisiana, USA). Migratory and dispersive, notoriously nomadic. Populations of Americas descended from immigrants from Europe that first arrived in 1880s and some transatlantic movement still occurs: one of four that arrived at Bermuda airport in Sept 2013 had been ringed as a chick the same year in Doñana, Spain. The species is a relatively recent colonist of the Americas. It reached North America, occupying the Atlantic coast, thereafter spreading N and along Gulf coast, especially since the 1940s, and has recently colonized E Canada, where the first record was in 1986. In the Caribbean, it is fairly common in Greater Antilles and apparently increasing. Records of birds in transit or in winter have become more frequent in Mexico, where strong evidence of breeding was first obtained in 1988. Also reported increasingly in Central America, where it nests in Costa Rica, and in N South America, notably in Colombia, presumably as a result of the increased numbers in North America and West Indies (Matheu *et al.,* 2018).

[54] **Order: CATHARTIFORMES**: Chesser, *et al.*, 2016 recognized new orders Steatornithiformes, Nyctibiiformes, and Cathartiformes.

[55] **Black Vulture** (*Coragyps atratus atratus*): Status established as Partial Migrant (PM), Garrido and Kirkconnell, 2011 treated this species as Very Rare without any Resident Status. Posteriorly González *et al*, 2013 found a small population in Sierra de Bibanasí, Matanzas province in mid-July and a sighting of one immature individual, which could suggest the possibility that the species is breeding in the area. Nesting is not confirmed yet; further studies are needed.

[56] **Osprey (*carolinensis*)** (*Pandion haliaetus carolinensis*): There is one record of this race breeding in Cuba (Kirkconnell and Garrido, 1997), but an isolated record is not enough to consider the population as a breeding resident yet.

[57] **Cuban Kite** (*Chondrohierax wilsonii*): Until recently was considered conspecific with *C. uncinatus*, but trend is now widespread to accept full species status. The Cuban Kite differs because of its all-yellow larger bill; barred collar and underparts pattern; and smaller overall size (del Hoyo *et al.*, 2018). Molecular evidence also supports this split (Johnson *et al.*, 2007). I disagree with the not accepted species status of the Cuban population in the 49th Supplement of AOU, so I decided to consider the above evidence as valid, and give it the status of full species.

[58] **Bare-legged Owl** (*Margarobyas lawrencii exsul*): At times treated as Monotypic. Birds from western Cuba and Isle of Pines are sometimes separated as race *exsul*, but apparently indistinguishable from those in rest of range (Holt *et al.,* 2018).

[59] **Burrowing Owl (Florida)** (*Athene cunicularia*): Other populations have been found on different parts of the island; further studies are necessary to clarify its taxonomic status. Definitely there are resident populations (*A. c. guantanamensis* from the east, and the western population *A. cunicularia. ssp (insertae sedis)* which are pending clarification of their subspecific status), and migratory populations; birds belonging to the North American subspecies (*floridana*) have been seen regularly in the northern keys of Cuba during fall migration. Regalado, 1975 suggested that some specimens shared the same measurements as *A. c. hypugea* from northwestern North America.

[60] **Short-eared Owl (Antillean)** (*Asio flammeus domingensis*): Race *domingensis* was formerly considered a separate species (Garrido, 1995), including *portoricensis* (and later also *cubensis*) as a race. Alternatively, *domingensis* and *portoricensis* have been considered a single race of present species. Species status has not been accepted.

[61] **West Indian Woodpecker** (*Melanerpes superciliaris spp*): Around the Isle of Youth, proposed races

sanfelipensis (Cayo Real, in Cayos de San Felipe) and *florentinoi* (Cayo Largo) both considered inseparable, and both populations may now be extinct (Winkler *et al.*, 2018). Five subspecies recognized.

[62] **Cuban Green Woodpecker** (*Xiphidiopicus percussus spp*): Six races have been named, but species exhibit considerable variation in size and coloration throughout range, and much overlap in characteristics among different populations; thus, described races *monticola* (E Cuba) and *cocoensis* (Cayo Coco and nearby cays) are regarded as synonyms of nominate race, and *gloriae* (Cantiles Keys) and *marthae* (Cayo Caballones) as synonyms of *insulaepinorum*. Two subspecies currently recognized (Winkler *et al.*, 2018).

[63] **Northern Flicker (Cuban)** (*Colaptes auratus chrysocaulosus*): Sometimes called Yellow-shafted Flicker (HBW Alive, 2018). Races *chrysocaulosus* and *gundlachi* are morphologically close to *auratus* and clearly belong with this species, although the former is sometimes treated as a separate species (Winkler *et al.*, 2018).

[64] **Ivory-billed Woodpecker (Cuban)** (*Campephilus principalis bairdii*): Fleischer *et al.*, 2006 found some molecular evidence to split the Cuban population as a full species. Morphologically, however, it is close to nominate; this assumption has not been accepted by any recognized international list.

[65] **Crested Caracara** (*Caracara cheriway audubonii*): Usually treated as conspecific with *C. plancus*, but recently split from former and sometimes treated as Monotypic. Northern birds have been separated as race *audubonii* (described from Florida), but claimed differences in plumage tone appear to be due to wear, and those of size to clinal variation. (del Hoyo *et al.*, 2018).

[66] **American Kestrel (Cuban)** (*Falco sparverius sparverioides*): Occasionally considered a Cuban endemic (at subspecific level), but the race is also known in Bahamas and Jamaica.

[67] **Red-and-green Macaw** (*Ara chloropterus*): Recently established with local breeding populations, the three species move in mixed flocks; hybridization has been recorded, further studies are required.

[68] **Scarlet Macaw** (*Ara macao ssp.*): Recently established with local breeding populations, the three species move in mixed flocks; hybridization has been recorded, further studies are required.

[69] **Blue-and-yellow Macaw** (*Ara ararauna*): Recently established with local breeding populations, the three species move in mixed flocks; hybridization has been recorded, further studies are required.

[70] **Giant Kingbird** (*Tyrannus cubensis*): Previously considered endemic (*de facto*) of Cuba (Raffaelle *et al.*, 1998, Birdlife International, 2016, Navarro and Reyes, 2017), because of its presumed local extirpation from south Bahamas and the Turks and Caicos (Birdlife International, 2016). I decided not to consider this species as endemic to Cuba as there are no currently recognized categories for the endemic concept, and the species has a previous wider distributional pattern, where other native and self-sustaining populations were known, but became extinct recently.

[71] **Cuban Pewee** (*Contopus caribaeus ssp*): Status of form *florentinoi* (Cayo Anclitas, off southern Cuba) unclear, and date of description uncertain; possibly valid, provisionally included in *nerlyi* (Farnsworth and Lebbin, 2018).

[72] **Alder Flycatcher** (*Empidonax alnorum*): Alder and Willow Flycatchers are perhaps among the more difficult birds to identify in the area (Phillips, 1948). The best fields marks used to differentiate them are the vocalizations and/or using a few morphometric parameters (wing formulas) (Pyle, 1997 and Colorado, 2013), which usually overlap depending on the populations (Seutin, 1991). The Cuban material referring to "Traill´s Flycatcher" was originally identified as *Empidonax trailli* and there was an unclear situation related to the two specimens collected by Orlando Garrido in the Havana Botanical Garden (the previous one) with Catalog Number: IES-1463 (IB-1463 Instituto de Biología), 4 October, 1966 (specimen removed from the collection due its poor degree of conservation) and the other IES-1947, from La Vega, Isle of Youth (15 October, 1967).
I personally reviewed the specimen from La Vega, Isle of Youth with Catalog Number: IES-1947 (IB-Instituto de Biología) collected by Orlando Garrido, 15 October, 1967, with notes written by James Bond (J.B.) and A. R. Phillips (ARP). One of the two labels attached to the specimen said: *Empidonax t. traillii J.B* and on the back: "*OK. traillii, sensu A.O.U, axantic mutant, probably <u>alnorum</u> but Wing rounded as in traillii = "campestris" ARP ´67*". *Empidonax alnorum* was first mentioned for Cuba by Bond (1968) and later considered valid by Garrido and Kirkconnell, 2011. It is interesting that Bond, 1985 mentioned Traill´s Flycatcher (*Empidonax trailli*), listing it as a Vagrant for the West Indies (including Cuba and Jamaica), and never again mentioned *E. alnorum*. Llanes and Navarro (*in prep.*) carefully measured this specimen and calculated the wing formulas

following Pyle, 1997. They concluded that it matched with a high degree of confidence the range of Alder Flycatcher (R >2.91) (Pyle, 1997 and Colorado, 2013) resulting as R=4.22. For this reason I decided to validate the record of Alder Flycatcher for Cuba.

[73] **Willow Flycatcher** (*Empidonax traillii*): The references given for this species for Cuba (Bond, 1985; Garrido and García, 1975 and Garrido and Kirkconnell, 2011) were based on the specimens collected by Garrido in the previous Havana Botanical Garden (IES-1463, now removed from the collection due its high degree of damage) and La Vega, Isle of Youth (IES-1947). The latter was previously identified as *E. trailli* by James Bond, as is written on one of the labels; A. R. Phillips gave it an unclear status *alnorum/trailli* (*campestris*). Recently Llanes and Navarro (*in prep.*) placed it in the morphometric range of *alnorum* following Pyle, 1997, giving clarification to the status of this sample. As the specimen from Havana (IES-1463) was removed due to its poor conservation (Jorge Luis Guerra com pers., 2018) it was not possible to determine any taxonomic status, just considered it "Traill´s Flycatcher", following Pyle, 1997.
The first reliable record of Willow Flycatcher (*Empidonax trailli*) was one specimen captured in a mist net in the banding station in Guanahacabibes, Pinar del Río province, western Cuba (Llanes and Navarro, en prep). It was clearly identified using the wing formula following Pyle, 1997 (Llanes *et al.*, 2016).

[74] **Least Flycatcher** (*Empidonax minimus*): The first mention of this species was made by González, *et al.*, 2006; but apparently the authors were unaware that it was the first record of the species for Cuba. Posteriorly Rodríguez *et al.*, 2014 mentioned it again, just referring to it as part of a group of birds restricted to the Sabana-Camaguey Archipelago. The bird was captured in a mist net and banded in an evergreen forest in Cayo Santa María 14 October 2001, identified and banded by Alejandro Llanes using the wing formula, following Pyle, 1997.

[75] **Vermilion Flycatcher (Northern)** (*Pyrocephalus rubinus (prob. blatteus)*: Recent molecular analysis suggests that *P. rubinus* (Austral Vermilion Flycatcher) could be a Monotypic species separated from the other northern forms. The other populations (to which the Cuban specimen must pertain) could be split into a full and Polytypic species under *P. obscurus* (Common Vermilion Flycatcher) (Carmi *et al.*, 2016).

[76] **Cuban Vireo** (*Vireo gundlachii sspp*): Races rather poorly differentiated; species sometimes treated as monotypic (Brewer *et al.*, 2018). The species has been recorded in Florida in 2016 and 2017 (Chesser *et al.*, 2018). Some authors have treated it as conspecific with *V. griseus*.

[77] **Bank Swallow** (*Riparia riparia riparia*): Status changed to Winter Resident (WR)-Transient (T), formerly considered as Transient (T) (Garrido and Kirckonnell, 2011). eBird, 2018 sightings show that the species is present in Cuba in winter months.

[78] **Barn Swallow (American)** (*Hirundo rustica erythrogaster*): Status changed to Winter Resident (WR)-Transient (T), formerly considered Transient (T) (Garrido and Kirckonnell, 2011). eBird, 2018 sightings show that the species is wintering in Cuba.

[79] **Swainson's Thrush (Olive-backed)** (*Catharus ustulatus swainsoni*): Sometimes *swainsoni* is treated as a full species (del Hoyo *et al.*, 2018). Status change to Winter Resident (WR) and Transient (T), eBird, 2018 sightings show they also stay in Cuba during the winter months; previously considered just Transient.

[80] **Red-legged Thrush (plumbeus/schistaceus)** (*Turdus plumbeus sspp*): Some lists consider the Cuban populations as different from the Bahamian populations. Northern Red-legged Thrush (*Turdus plumbeus*) (Monotypic), is given the status of full species, whereas Western Red-legged Thrush (*Turdus rubripes*) including races *rubripes* and *schistaceus* are recognized in Cuba, and *coryi* in Cayman Brac. Different lists consider *schistaceus* as a race of *plumbeus*, and *rubripes* and *coryi* are treated as conspecifics. Further studies are required to clarify the status of these populations (del Hoyo *et al.*, 2018).

[81] **Tricolored Munia** (*Lonchura malacca ssp.*): Sometimes considered Monotypic (Payne, 2018).

[82] **American Pipit (rubescens/pacificus)** (*Anthus rubescens rubescens*): Also called Buff-bellied Pipit (HBW Alive, 2018). The specimens from Cuba appear to pertain to the nominate subspecies.

[83] **Lapland Longspur** (*Calcarius lapponicus lapponicus*): Subspecies amended. Martínez *et al.* 2016, referred to the specimen photographed in Cuba as belonging to the race *subcalcaratus* (described from Greenland), without any comment about diagnosis or similarities with the bird in the pictures presented in Martínez *et al.* 2016. Subspecies *subcalcaratus* appears to be a clinal variation and had been treated as a synonym of *lapponicus*. Three subspecies have been recognized: *lapponicus* and *alascensis* occurred in North America, and

coloratus in Eurasia.
Further analysis of the pictures in Martínez *et al.* 2016, revealed that it more probably belongs to the nominal subspecies *lapponicus*. It shows extensive black on the sides and dark above; race *alascensis* is paler than nominate, black reduced, supercilium more ochre-tinged, bill large and more streaked above; *coloratus* is larger, darker above with extensive rusty color on the wings (Rising & Christie, 2018).

[84] **Yellow-headed Warbler** (*Teretistris fernandinae*): A contact area was discovered recently along the southern coast between Cienfuegos and Trinidad. Hybridization process has been argued for intermediate individuals; many specimens found frequently in the contact zone (see eBird Yellow-headed x Oriente Warbler).

[85] **Oriente Warbler** (*Teretistris fornsi fornsi*): A contact area was discovered recently along the southern coast between Cienfuegos and Trinidad. Hybridization process has been argued for intermediate individuals, many specimens found frequently in the contact zone.

[86] **Oriente Warbler** (*Teretistris fornsi turquinensis*): Sometimes treated as Monotypic. Birds from Pico Turquino, in SW of range, recently proposed as race *turquinensis*, allegedly slightly larger and longer-tailed than others, also darker, more sooty grey on crown and upperparts and with grey (rather than brownish) wash on rear flanks; further study required (Curson, 2018 a).

[87] **Hooded Oriole** (*Icterus cucullatus cf. igneus*): Gundlach (1873) mentioned this species placing it in the Series II (the ones that come from "America Septentrional") following d´Orbigny (1837-1856) distribution patterns and commenting that "it is a very rare visitor to the island during the spring". Only two records have been found for Cuba (Garrido and García, 1975). One specimen is located in the Bird collection of the Felipe Poey Museum, University of Havana (specimen MFP.13.001315); an adult male in breeding plumage collected at El Cerro, Havana, 5 November, 1932. The other specimen is located in the Gundlach collection with a catalog number: IES-113 (Instituto de Ecología y Sistemática). The former specimen (Gundlach) is mounted and in a poor degree of conservation, labeled as: "*Icterus cucullatus* ♂, Turpial; Introducido". The bird is not a Hooded Oriole, instead it is a Baltimore Oriole (*Icterus galbula*). I don´t know why the specimen was misidentified. Originally the Gundlach collection contained four species of Orioles: one *Icterus* sp. No. 198 (identified posteriorly as *I. galbula*), three *Icterus spurius* No.133 (x2) and No. 233 (x1), *Xanthornus hypomelas* (=*Icterus dominiscensis*) No. 1, and one *Icterus cucullatus*, No. 113 (Ragues, 1914).

[88] **Red-shouldered Blackbird** (*Agelaius assimilis subniger*): Birds from Isle of Youth formerly separated as a geographical race, *subniger* are not considered a valid form as the description was based on immature specimens. Sometimes treated as Monotypic (Fraga, 2018).

[89] **Northern Waterthrush** (*Parkesia noveboracensis sspp.*): Sometimes considered Politypic, geographical variation perhaps mostly clinal, and racial differences somewhat obscured by individual variation. Birds from Newfoundland described as race *fuliginosus* have been considered inseparable from nominate (Curson, 2018 b).

[90] **Tennessee Warbler** (*Oreothlypis peregrina*): This species has been treated under new genus *Leiothlypis* (HBW Alive) following Sangster, 2008 by other international lists.

[91] **Orange-crowned Warbler (celata)** (*Oreothlypis celata celata*): This species has been treated under new genus *Leiothlypis* (HBW Alive) following Sangster, 2008 by other international lists.

[92] **Nashville Warbler (ruficapilla)** (*Oreothlypis ruficapilla ruficapilla*): This species has been treated under new genus *Leiothlypis* (HBW Alive, 2018) following Sangster, 2008 by other international lists.

[93] **Virginia's Warbler** (*Oreothlypis virginiae*): The register of the species was made in 1992 by Wunderle *et al.* (1992). The senior author (who is an experienced and recognized ornithologist) saw the bird 2 March, 1989 in the vicinity of Gamboa, Majana, now Artemisa province (western Cuba) giving a detailed description of the bird where field marks were evident; he could see the bird for about five minutes (Wunderle *et al.*, 1992). Vagrant birds have been found in the east of North America as far as north as Newfoundland and south to Atlanta (eBird, 2018). There have been sightings in closer areas such as Grand Bahama and Grand Abaco.

[94] **American Redstart** (*Setophaga ruticilla*): There is only one official record of the species breeding in Cuba (Kirkconnell and Garrido, 1996), which is why it cannot be considered a breeding species.

[95] **Olive-capped Warbler** (*Setophaga pityophila*): Birds from Bahamas described as race *bahamensis* on the

basis of longer tail and other differences in morphology; they tend also to be darker, more plumbeous-grey on upperparts, yellower on forecrown, less heavily marked with black around yellow throat and breast, and greyer on flanks. Possibly worthy of recognition, but further study required; recent study found relatively little genetic variation among populations (Curson, 2018).

[96] **Yellow-rumped Warbler (Audubon´s)** (*Setophaga coronata auduboni*): Considered a full species called Audubon´s Warbler (*S. auduboni*) by different international authoritative bird lists (see HBW Alive, 2018). A recent genetic study proposed that at least *S. coronata*, *S. auduboni* and *goldmani* should be treated as species. This separation was not validated by Chesser *et al.*, 2011.

[97] **Yellow-throated Warbler** (*Setophaga dominica sspp.*): Sometimes treated as Monotypic (see HBW Alive, 2018). Recent work has suggested that the three generally recognized races are so weakly differentiated, with variation primarily clinal, that they should be combined as one, especially as there is no genetic support for any of them; consequently *albilora* (described from Belize, but breeds W of Appalachian Mts) and *stoddardi* (Walton County, Florida), as well as proposed race *axantha* (from Ohio), are all considered inseparable (Curson, 2018).

[98] **Black-throated Gray Warbler** (*Setophaga nigrescens sspp.*): Two subspecies recognized (*nigrescens* and *halsseii*). Race *halseii* with subtle differences in the grey of the upperparts has been considered invalid by some authors, although nucleotide-sequence divergence between the two races is similar to that between *S. townsendi* and *S. occidentalis*. The individual observed in Cuba was not referred to subspecific level; perhaps it belongs to the nominal subspecies (Curson, 2018).

[99] **Canada Warbler** (*Cardellina canadensis*): There is only one supposed wintering record 2 February 2003 (Craves and Hall, 2003); therefore it is treated here as a Transient.

[100] **Indigo Bunting** (*Passerina cyanea*): Castaneda and Wiley, 2015 recorded the probable first breeding register of the species in Cuba. A local "pajarero" (bird-trapper) found a couple of adult (male and female) Indigo Buntings, and caught three fledglings in Ciego de Avila, July 2012. Further studies required to definitely modify its breeding status in Cuba. Subsequently the resident status must change also.

[101] **Saffron Finch** (*Sicalis flaveola*): The first mention of this species was made by Gundlach, 1873 using an old synonym *Crithagra brasiliensis* (*Fringilla*); Gundlach also said that a male was trapped in a backyard in Matanzas in 1853, where it was possible to see other individuals in cages in surrounding areas. Later, Garrido, 1997 reported the Saffron Finch in Cuba for the first time; probably Garrido was unaware of the Gundlach citation because an older synonym was used: *Crithagra brasiliensis=Sicalis flaveola*. Recently Yaroddy Rodríguez (com. pers., 2018) sent me a picture of a caged Saffron Finch that he bought from a person who captured it three years ago in San Antonio de los Baños, near Havana. Rodríguez also mentioned to me that he knew a person who brought some Saffron Finches from Guyana to breed them and later released a flock into the wild in the surrounding areas of the cemetery, in the town proper of San Antonio de los Baños. Current status of this population is unknown.

[102] **Blue-black Grassquit** (*Volatinia jacarina splendens*): Garrido and Montaña (1967, 1968 and 1975) mentioned that an adult male bird was owned by a local "pajarero" (bird trapper) Silvio Lizalde, who had received the bird from another *pajarero* in Pinar del Río, who said he had trapped it in the vicinity of Candelaria, Pinar del Río Province, using a cage and a decoy. It was not considered a vagrant as it showed symptoms of having been in captivity for a long time (Garrido and Montaña, 1975) and by the scant knowledge of the migration process at the time (Garrido, com pers, 2018). The fact that it is very common and widespread in Middle America in areas as close as Yucatan and it is not a typical caged bird in the international bird trade, along with sightings of other Middle American birds in Cuba could support the presence of this bird in the western province of Cuba as a Vagrant. Hurricanes and other meteorological processes sometimes "trap" birds and force them to move into other surrounding areas. It is interesting to note that in 1966, hurricane Alma originated in central America, went through the western Caribbean and hit Cuba in the western extreme (Pinar del Río), extending clouds and winds over an area of 520, 000 km^2. The hurricane also affected continental zones of the Caribbean coast and Yucatán at the same time.

[103] **Cuban Grassquit** (*Tiaris canorus*): At times the genus *Phonipara* has been resurrected to refer to this species following molecular evidence, and it is not considered similar to *Tiaris olivaceus* (Burns *et al.* 2016 and Rising, 2018).

[104] **Black-faced Grassquit** (*Tiaris bicolor bicolor*): Sometimes placed in the genus *Melanospiza* (see HBW Alive, 2018). Previously applied only to St Lucia Black Finch (*M. richardsoni*) (in HBW, 2018), molecular evidence

extends it to *M. bicolor*; both species have pink legs and feet and dark plumage without facial markings (Rising, 2018).

[105] **Cuban Bullfinch** (*Melopyrrha nigra*): Sometimes assigned to *Pyrrhulagra* (see HBW Alive, 2018). More recently considered an objective junior synonym for *Loxigilla* and is unavailable as a genus name for the group containing *portoricensis*, *nigra*, and *violacea* based on genetic data (Chesser *et al.*, 2018). I consider as valid the separation of *nigra* from *taylori* (Garrido *et al.*, 2014) based on morphological characters and vocalizations. This proposal was rejected by Chesser *et al.*, 2016.

[106] **Greater Scaup** (*Aythya marila nearctica*): Hypothetical. Bond, 1950 mentioned a record from Western Cuba (Lake Ariguanao, Morales) and Garrido observed one individual in the artificial channel Caleta del Sábalo, Zapata Swamp, 16 January 1968 (Garrido and García, 1975). He shot but missed the target (Garrido, com pers. 2018). Bond (1950) said that as the specimen from Western Cuba could not be located, he assumed that identification error could happen. The species had also been recorded (apparently identified from a captured bird) in Bahamas, Watling´s Island and Run Cay (Bond, 1950).

[107] **Common Goldeneye** (*Bucephala clangula*): A hypothetical species mentioned as *"Clangula glaucion americana* Bd. Bwr. & Ridgw. Hist. N. Am. W. Bds. II, p. 44 (1884) (Cuba) (?)... Recorded from Cuba and Barbuda... *Op cit.*"

Bond, 1945 mentioned in the *Check-List of Birds of the West Indies*:

*"...Records of the following North American species are considered unsatisfactory: Cygnus sp. (Antigua), Branta canadensis (Andros, New Providence, Jamaica, Barbados), Branta bernicla (Barbados), Bucephala clangula (Bahama Islands, Cuba, Barbados), Oidemia perspicillata (Jamaica), Mergus merganser (Cuba). All of the above are known from Florida and may occur at times in the West Indies. In addition, Anas penelope, Clangula hyemalis, Oidemia fusca and O. nigra may eventually be reported from this region...*Op cit.*

Many of this species have already been registered for the Antilles. There have been more than 50 sightings of Common Goldeneye on the southern coast of United States; about 20 sightings were made in the Florida area (eBird, 2018).

[108] **Black Swift (borealis)** (*Cypseloides niger borealis*): Hypothetical sighting. Llanes *et al.* 2016 mentioned that individuals were seen in a mixed flock with Chimney Swifts, during the days of peak fall migration around the lighthouse in Cabo de San Antonio, western part of Cuba, which suggests it could pertain to the North American form:
"Al parecer, los individuos observados en el Cabo de San Antonio provienen de las poblaciones de esta especie que se reproducen en Norteamérica... (referring to *borealis*) *...y pasan el invierno en Centroamérica, ya que las residentes permanentes en Cuba, según Garrido y Kirkconnell (2011), se encuentran en la parte central y oriental del país..."*; they also suggested *"...De ahí que puede ser considerada además esta especie (subspecies) para Cuba como raro transeúnte local." Op. cit.*

[109] **Blue Jay** (*Cyanocitta cristata*): A hypothetical sighting, there is one unconfirmed sighting from La Turba, Zapata Swamp, 23 November, 2018. The observer Jocelyn Pelletier reported seeing the bird while birding with a small group of birders; she mentioned that as a North American she recognizes a Blue Jay very well as it is a common bird there. The Blue Jay is a conspicuous bird, impossible to confuse with any other Cuban bird. Pelletier was accompanied by other members of the group and a local guide, Mario, who works in the National Park. The lack of graphic material supporting this sighting prevents us from validating it with eBird (ebird.org ID=S50150569).

[110] **Pine Siskin** (*Spinus pinus*): d´Orbigny (1837-1856) mentioned *Carduelis pinus* (= *Spinus pinus*) as fairly common in Cuba, especially near Havana during the winter. Posteriorly Gundlach, 1873 mentioned this species (*Chrysomitris pinus*) denying its presence and assuming a probable confusion with Lesser Goldfinch (*Spinus psaltria*) which was the bird he found in Havana at the time. As there is no other reference of its presence in Cuba, I decided to place it as hypothetical. d´Orbigny made a very detailed description of this bird which matches perfectly with Pine Siskin (*S. pinus*) (see d´Orbigny, 1837-1856 pp. 85-86). The Lesser Goldfinch absolutely lacks any streaks on the underparts as described by d´Orbigny for the birds he saw and collected; he also provided measurements of different parts (d´Orbigny, 1837-1856, p. 85). Pine Siskin is considered a Resident and/or Partial Migrant in North America. It is an irruptive and highly nomadic bird in autumn and winter; banding suggests erratic or highly variable movements throughout the year. Straggler visitor on Pribilof Islands, Aleutian Island (Unimai), and islands in the Bering Sea. Vagrant in S Baja California, in Bermuda, and at sea in N Atlantic Ocean (on board E-bound ship c. 3060 km E of New York). An adult, possibly of nominate race, was recorded on the Arctic coast of Chukotka, NE Russia, in Jun 2011 (Clement and

Juana, 2018).

[111] **Connecticut Warbler** (*Oporornis agilis*): Hypothetical. It was mentioned as "*very rare migrant in Bahamas, Cuba, Hispaniola...*" in Raffaelle *et al.* 1998, *A Guide to the Birds of the West Indies*. Actually there is no official publication or eBird observation to support this sighting for Cuba, even though the species has been recorded for the islands around Cuba. Garrido (com pers. 2018) referred to sighting one individual of a supposed Connecticut/Mourning Warbler in the previous Havana Botanical Garden in 1964, the bird was foraging on the ground, and he tried to collect it but the bird flew as he approached. As the sighting remains unclear, I decided to place it as a hypothetical record.

[112] **Yellow-tailed Oriole** (*Icterus mesomelas ssp.*): Reported mistakenly as pertaining to the Gundlach collection in Navarro and Reyes, 2017. It was found by Orlando Garrido (Garrido com pers., 2018) in the Ramsden´s collection (currently in Santiago de Cuba) and mentioned by James Bond as "Cuba; specimen examined" (Bond, 1950), but given an uncertain status. Efforts to find this specimen in the Ramsden collection were unsatisfactory; for this reason I decided to consider it a hypothetical species.

[113] **Rusty Blackbird** (*Euphagus carolinus*): There was a visual sighting of a supposed bird like a *Euphagus* sp. (probably *E. carolinus*) in the previous Havana Botanical Garden (Garrido and García, 1975). I personally asked Garrido (Garrido com pers. 2018) and he suggested placing it as hypothetical because he had no further details; the bird was too high up in the palm tree to allow him to make an accurate identification of the species.

[114] **Northern Cardinal** (*Cardinalis cardinalis ssp.*): Recently, in 2007, Osmani Carrillo Chaviano, who was working as a forest ranger in Cayo Santa María, commented to the ornithologist Edwin Ruiz Rojas (com pers. 2018) that he had seen a completely red, crested bird with a red bill and black behind the bill in Cayo Ensenachos. It happened in the Hotel Iberostar Ensenachos in between the tennis courts and the bungalow. This matches perfectly with the field marks of the Northern Cardinal, no other bird has the same field marks, at least in this area. Carrillo reported that he didn´t remember the exact dates, but said it was the beginning of the cold season (prob. October-November); the bird was foraging in the small bushes in the garden, also a typical behavior of this bird. Gundlach, 1873 citing Poey, mentioned that the species (*Cardinalis virginianus= Cardinalis cardinalis*) is common in cages brought from North America. Gundlach himself saw an individual in January 1860. Later, he learned that it had escaped from captivity in the neighborhood. The sighting on the northern key could be a vagrant bird from North America. Currently, Northern Cardinal is not a caged bird in Cuba, and there are no people living on this key; it is just a touristic area.

[115] **Painted Bunting** (*Passerina ciris pallidior*): Hypothetical species. Painting Buntings breed in two allopatric eastern and western breeding populations separated by at least 550 km at their closest point (Thompson, 1991). They were described as two separate subspecies (Mears, 1911). Races differ significantly in migration and molting strategies. Further research suggested molecular differences between them (Herr, 2011). Both subspecies are poorly differentiated making it difficult to distinguish color and morphology, race *pallidior* is larger and paler than nominate. Storer, 1951 failed to find consistent differences between eastern and western birds. A proposal to validate *pallidior* as a different species (Tweit, 2014) was rejected by Chesser *et al.*, 2015. The author has seen birds trapped by *pajareros* in Gibara, Holguín province that match the paler color pattern of the western populations. Because of the lack of consistent field marks of both races, these sightings should be considered hypothetical for now; further studies are required.

[116] **Village Weaver** (*Ploceus cucullatus*): Hypothetical. Kirkconnell *et al.*, 2005 included this species on a list for Zapata Swamp. This sighting lacks any information, just the author´s mention on the list with the following categories: *Accidental, Very Rare,* and *Forest areas* as the habitat, without any other comment. There is no official paper registering the species for Cuba, no photographs, videos or any other visual material to support the record. I asked Orestes Martínez (El Chino Zapata, a recognized Cuban birding guide) for further data; he said that his brother Angel saw a bird supposedly belonging to this species, but it could not be verified.

[117] **Tinamou (not specified)** (Tinamidae *sp.*): Bond, 1950 mentioned that Tinamous were introduced to Pinar del Río, Cuba, from Mexico in late 1931, remarking that, at this time, the introduction evidently failed. There are four species of Tinamous in Mexico; Great Tinamou (*Tinamus major*) is probably the most commonly known because of its larger size, but it was not specified.

[118] **Plain Chachalaca** (*Ortalis vetula*), **California Quail** (*Callipepla californica*), **Montezuma Quail** (*Cyrtonyx montezumae*) **and Barbary Partridge** (*Alectoris barbara*): Species first mentioned by Bond, 1950 and later by Garrido and Montaña, 1975 as introduced without satisfactory self-sustaining populations; now have become extinct.

[119] **Ocelated Turkey** (*Meleagris ocellata*): Bond, 1950 mentioned that Ocelated Turkey (*Agriocharis*= *Meleagris*) was introduced in Pinar del Río, Cuba, from Mexico in late 1931, remarking that, at the time, the introduction evidently failed.

[120] **Wood Rail (not specified)** (*Aramides sp.*): Bond, 1950 mentioned that Wood Rails (*Aramides*) were introduced in Pinar del Río, Cuba, from Mexico in late 1931, remarking that, at the time, the introduction evidently failed. Only two species of this genus inhabit Mexico: *A. axilaris* and *A. albiventris*.

[121] **Thick-knee (not specified)** (*Burhinus sp.*): Bond, 1950 mentioned that Thick-knees (*Burhinus*) were introduced in Pinar del Río, Cuba, from Mexico in late 1931, remarking that, at the time, the introduction evidently failed. As in Mexico there is only one species. Bond very probably referred to the Double-striped Thick-knee (*Burhinus bistriatus*).

[122] **Common Kingfisher (Common)** (*Alcedo atthis ssp.*): Removed from the main list as the origin of this sighting is controversial, considering that it is a Eurasian species and not potentially part of the Cuban fauna.

[123] **Rosy-faced Lovebird** (*Agapornis roseicollis ssp.*): Amended identification. It has been mentioned before as *personatus* (Navarro and Reyes, 2017), but analysis of the photographs reviewed revealed that the sighting belongs to *roseicollis*.

[124] **House Crow** (*Corvus splendens ssp.*): Removed from the main list. One individual was registered in Cayo Guillermo, Cuba; there are pictures of the bird in breeding behavior holding twigs in its bill. The bird has not been observed since hurricane Irma in 2017(Paulino López Delgado, com pers., 2018). The bird supposedly reached the key on a commercial or cruise ship that usually travels along the Bahama Channel (Paulino López Delgado com pers, 2018).

[125] **Eurasian Blackcap** (*Sylvia atricapilla ssp.*): Removed from the main list. As it is a Eurasian species with infrequent sightings in North America and the fact that it was a caged bird reported by a local bird trapper as captured in the wild could generate controversies, I decided to remove it from the main list until further data could clarify its status.

[126] **Scarlet-faced Liocichla** (*Liocichla ripponi*): Identification amended. The specimen was originally identified by Rodríguez *et al.*, 2017 as pertaining to Red-faced Liocichla (*L. phoenicea*). *L. ripponi* was treated as conspecific with *Liocichla phoenicea* and raised to specific level based on morphological and molecular characters (Mays *et al.*, 2015). The pictures of the individual reported in the paper clearly pertain to *L. ripponi*. The field marks are: *ripponi* differs from *phoenicea* in having the crimson on the face and black lateral crown-stripe replaced by much brighter scarlet extending clearly over the eye, onto the lores, and over the malar area onto the chin. Crown grey, upperparts greyer, underparts markedly paler and buffy-greyer, undertail buffy-grey with an orange wash, whereas *phoenicea* is bronzy-red, and has a longer tail (Collar, 2011).

[127] **Crested Myna** (*Acridotheres cristatellus ssp.*): Not referred to any subspecific level. In the picture that appeared in the paper reporting the bird for Cuba (Rodríguez *et al.* 2017), the feathers of the crest look narrower as in the race *brevipennis* which is also the one recorded in other countries around the world. In North America, the species has been recorded as introduced in Vancouver, Canada.

[128] **Rufous-collared Sparrow** (*Zonotricia capensis ssp.*): Reported as "trapped" (probably escaped from captivity) in Garrido and García, 1975. The specimen belongs to the Bauzá historic collection, now in the National Museum of Natural History in Havana, with the number MNHNC 80-000434. The original label attached to the side of the wooden base said *521* (written with red ink) and in capitals "*Cogido el 26 Noviembre 1935. En un parque del Cerro.-Comprado "Mercado Único" el 12 Diciembre.* ♀. *Huevera* (local word supposedly referring to the status of the female reproductive organs)." *4 Febrero-1936.*" Numerous races have been proposed, but many are poorly differentiated. Twenty-five subspecies have been recognized. No idea to which race it pertains, but definitely it is not close to *antillarum* form from Hispaniola, because of the lack of a continuous black collar around the throat.

[129] **European Goldfinch** (*Carduelis carduelis ssp.*): European species. Gundlach, 1873 mentioned that he found this species breeding around "Castillo del Principe", Havana. Later Bond, 1950 reported it in Güines, Cuba and posteriorly Garrido and García, 1975 considered them "trapped birds" probably escaped from captivity based on the previous mentions.

[130] **Lesser Goldfinch**/*Spinus psaltria jouyi*: Locally fairly common near Havana (Villalba), extending to the southern coast *a posteriori* (Bauzá) (Bond, 1950). Gundlach targeted a couple of individuals (mentioned under *Chrysomitris mexicana*) from a flock of about 15 birds in "La Quinta de los Molinos, Habana" in 1860 (Gundlach, 1873). He rejected the sighting of *Ch. pinus* (d´Orbigny, 1837-1856) considering the possibility of

confusion with *psaltria*. D´Orbigny also mentioned that it was a very common species in Cuba and in particular, in the Havana surroundings. Bond, 1950 apparently presumed that the Cuban populations could be native and not introduced, when he wrote "introduced (?)".

[131] **Red Siskin** (*Spinus cucullatus*): Gundlach (1873) reported that the species (*Pyrrhomitris cucullatus*, old synonym) was frequent as a caged bird in many homes, brought from Caracas (Venezuela), and perhaps one individual escaped from captivity and was trapped in the wild; the description was published under *Fringila cubae* by Guérin (Gundlach, 1873). Later mentioned by Garrido and Montaña, 1975 as "trapped birds" probably escaped from captivity. Native of Venezuela, Colombia and Trinidad; currently Endangered with a rapid decline in population as it was heavily collected for the international bird trade. Supposedly introduced to Cuba as a caged bird (Clement and Sharpe, 2018). Also found in Puerto Rico (1930s) where small numbers still persist (Raffaelle *et al.* 1998).

[132] **Red-crested Cardinal** (*Paroaria coronata*): d´Orbigny (1837-1856) noted that de la Sagra brought a specimen of *Paroaria cucullata* (an old synonym which probably referred to a Red-crested Cardinal (*P. coronata*) captured in the wild, but considered the high probability of the bird having escaped from captivity.

[133] **Red-cowled Cardinal** (*Paroaria dominicana*): A Brazilian species probably escaped from captivity. Mentioned by Gundlach (1873) referring to "de la Sagra´s book" in d´Orbigny (1837-1856). He also commented that one bird was captured in a garden-backyard in Matanzas in 1852. d´Orbigny (1837-1856) made a detailed description of the species from the specimen captured and owned in Cuba. Although he identified one bird that somebody captured in the wild, he expressed doubts about whether it could be native to Cuba, explaining that people frequently brought them from Brazil and Guayana, and suggesting that his specimen could have escaped from captivity. I could not clarify if Gundlach was referring to the same individual mentioned in d´Orbigny (1837-1856). There is no further information about his specimen, at least not in de la Sagra´s book.

[134] **Cinnamon-rumped Seedeater** (*Sporophila torqueola*): A Mexican species. A specimen located in the bird collection of the Felipe Poey Museum of Natural History, University of Havana, pertaining to the collection of Gastón Villalba, collected in the vicinity of Marianao, Havana (García-Lau and González, 2016). Bond, 1950 mentioned he examined this specimen and commented that he had never seen this Seedeater at Marianao. Probably escaped from captivity.

[135] **Sudan Golden Sparrow** (*Passer luteus*): Described as "trapped birds" by Garrido and García, 1975, probably escaped from captivity. The specimen is located in the bird collection of Gaston Villalba in the Felipe Poey Museum of Natural History, from the "Parque Zoológico de la Habana" (Havana Zoo) (García–Lau and González, 2016). I personally reviewed this specimen; the label did not specify if the bird belonged to the zoo collection or if it were captured in the zoo, as is written textually on the label: "FRINGILLIDAE, *Auripasser luteus*, ♂, May 7 (or May 1. It is not clear), 1943, preparado Sep.11, 1943, Parque Zoológico, Hab –Africa–".

[136] **Black winged/Yellow-crowned Bishop** (*Euplectes hordaceus/afer*): Identification amended; Garrido and Wiley, 2010 originally identified the female specimen in the Bauzá collection as Northern Red Bishop (Orange Bishop) (*Euplectes franciscanus*), currently located in the National Museum of Natural History in Havana (MNHNC catalog number B-486). They suspected and discussed the possibility of natural occurrence. The presence of a contrasted dark brown eyeline and darker upperparts and dark shaft streaks on flanks are important field marks that characterize *E. hordaceus/afer*; whereas *E. franciscanus* shows a plain side of the face lacking the dark brown eyeline, fewer dark streaks on the flanks and lighter upperparts. It is difficult to make an accurate identification because females and juveniles of those species are difficult to distinguish. The specimen shows darker wings, which could suggest it is similar to *hordaceus*. Yellow-crowned Bishop has been recorded as introduced with self-sustaining populations in Puerto Rico and Jamaica (Raffaelle *et al.* 1998). Both species (*hordaceus* and *afer*) are native to Africa. Definitive status of the Cuban specimen needs to be clarified.

[137] **Yellow-mantled Widowbird** (*Euplectes macroura macroura*): Rodríguez *et al.*, 2017 made the first record of the species for Cuba and the West Indies; they had a photograph of the immature molting individual, but it was not possible to establish a subspecific status. Later, I asked Rodríguez for further photographs as he kept the specimen in captivity; the individual showed adult plumage with the yellow mantle characteristic of the nominate subspecies.

Species added to the list in the previous issue of the Checklist (2017)

1. **Common Merganser** (*Mergus merganser*)
2. **Surf Scoter** (*Melanitta perspicillata*)
3. **Eurasian Widgeon** (*Anas penelope*)
4. **Bahama Woodstar** (*Calliphlox evelynae*)
5. **Great Shearwater** (*Ardenna gravis*)
6. **Franklin's Gull** (*Larus pipixcan*)
7. **Ruff** (*Calidris pugnax*)
8. **Lesser Black-backed Gull** (*Larus fuscus*)
9. **Cooper´s Hawk** (*Accipiter cooperii*)
10. **Mississippi Kite** (*Ictinia mississippiensis*)
11. **Swainson´s Hawk** (*Buteo Swainsoni*)
12. **Short-tailed Hawk** (*Buteo brachyurus*)
13. **Common Kingfisher** (*Alcedo atthis*)
14. **Red-and-green Macaw** (*Ara chloropterus*)
15. **Blue-and-yellow Macaw** (*Ara ararauna*)
16. **Scarlet Macaw** (*Ara macao*)
17. **Cassin´s Kingbird** (*Tyrannus vociferans*)
18. **Vermilion Flycatcher** (*Pyrocephalus rubinus*)
19. **House Crow** (*Corvus splendens*)
20. **Hermit Thrush** (*Catharus guttatus*)
21. **Eurasian Blackcap** (*Sylvia atricapilla*)
22. **American Pipit** (*Anthus rubescens*)
23. **Lapland Longspur** (*Calcarius lapponicus*)
24. **Dark-eyed Junco** (*Junco hyemalis*)
25. **Altamira Oriole** (*Icterus gularis*)
26. **Yellow-tailed Oriole** (*Icterus mesomelas*)
27. **Kirtland´s Warbler** (*Setophaga kirtlandii*)
28. **Black-throated Gray Warbler** (*Setophaga nigrescens*)
29. **Townsend's Warbler** (*Setophaga townsendi*)
30. **Blue-black Grassquit** (*Volatinia jacarina*)
31. **Rose-ringed Parakeet** (*Psittacula krameri*)
32. **White-eared Bubul** (*Pycnonotus leucotis*)
33. **Red-faced Liocichla** (*Liocichla phoenicea*); *identification amended (see Other exotics of uncertain origin species)*
34. **Red-billed Leiothrix** (*Leiothrix lutea*)
35. **Crested Myna** (*Acridotheres cristatellus*)
36. **White-winged Snowfinch** (*Montifringilla nivalis*)
37. **Orange Bishop** (*Euplectes franciscanus*); *identification amended (see Other exotics of uncertain origin species)*
38. **Yellow-mantled Widowbird** (*Euplectes macroura*)

Cuban Birds, Numbers and Percentages

Categories	Total Numbers	%	vs
Taxonomy			
• Orders	27	*100%*	total
• Families	72	*100%*	total
• Genus	223	*100%*	total
• Species	394	*100%*	total
○ Cuban species in relation to the West Indies	683 (WI)	*58%*	vs total West Indies species (including recent extinctions)
• Forms	456	*100%*	Total (species and subspecies)
Threatened			
• Threatened Species	45	*11%*	vs total Cuban species
○ Threatened Species in relation to the West Indies	117 (WI)	*38%*	vs total Threatened West Indies
• Extinct (in recent times)	2	*0.5%*	vs total Cuban species
Endemism			
• Endemic Family	1	*1%*	vs total of Cuban families
• Endemic Genus	7	*3%*	vs total of Cuban genus
• Cuban Endemics	27	*7%*	vs total Cuban species
• Endemic Subspecies	28	*100%*	total
• Other West Indian Endemics	22	*6%*	vs total Cuban species
• Cuban Endemics in relation to the West Indies	182 (WI)	*15%*	vs total West Indies Endemics
Abundance, Breeding and Resident			
• Common and Fairly Common	185	*47%*	vs total Cuban species
• Breeding Species	156	*39%*	vs total Cuban species
• Year Round (YR)	93	*23%*	vs total Cuban species
• Partial Migrants (PM)	57	*14%*	vs total Cuban species
• Winter Resident and Transients (WR-T)	99	*25%*	vs total Cuban species
• Summer Resident and Transients (SR-T)	8	*2%*	vs total Cuban species
• Transients (T)	37	*9%*	vs total Cuban species
• Vagrant (V)	84	*21%*	vs total Cuban species
• Total, Permanent Resident Component*	150	*38%*	YR+PM/Total number of Cuban birds
• Total, Migrant Component*	201	*51%*	WR+SR+T+PM/Total number of Cuban birds
Introduced			
• Introduced species	12	*3%*	vs total Cuban species
• Exotic species not already established, probably escaped from captivity or vagrants from introduced populations (not considered part of the Cuban avifauna)	33	-	-
Hypothetical species	10	-	-

*Cuban birds cannot be placed in a "black and white" context when we speak about a migrant or a year round component. There are forms (species and subspecies) showing both conditions. Some of them, like Ruddy Turnstone (*Arenaria interpres morinella*) formerly considered a Winter Resident in Cuba, remain Year Round in small numbers, while others like Sharp-shinned Hawk (*Accipiter striatus*) have a local Year Round population (*A. s. fringilloides*) and another migratory population (*A. s. velox*). That is why I decided to consider them as Components, hoping to achieve a better understanding of these phenomena. Partial Migrants (formerly considered as Bimodal Permanent Residents) are intended to be part migratory and part year round; that is why they need to be counted twice to calculate each component. In any case, the conditions are perhaps more difficult to understand than we expected.

References

Acosta, M. and O. Torres Fundora, 1996. Captura de un Coco Rojo (*Eudocimus ruber*; Aves: Threskiornitidae) al norte de Ciego de Ávila, Cuba. *El Pitirre*, 9(3), p 8.

American Ornithologists' Union (AOU) Committee, 2007. Committee on Classification and Nomenclature of Birds (North and Middle America) Policy on English Names of Birds. *The Auk* 124(4): 1472.

AOU, 1973. Thirty-Second Supplement to the American Ornithologists´ Union Check-list of North American Birds. *The Auk*, Vol. 90:411-419.

Baptista *et al.*, 2018 (Baptista, L.F., Trail, P.W., Horblit, H.M., Boesman, P. & Kirwan, G.M. (2018). Plain Pigeon (*Patagioenas inornata*). In: del Hoyo, J., Elliott, A., Sargatal, J., Christie, D.A. & de Juana, E. (eds.). *Handbook of the Birds of the World Alive*. Lynx Edicions, Barcelona. (retrieved from www.hbw.com/node/54138 on 21 September 2018).

BirdLife International. 2016. *Tyrannus cubensis*. The IUCN Red List of Threatened Species 2016: e.T22700516A93782366.http://dx.doi.org/10.2305/IUCN.UK.2016-3.RLTS.T22700516A93782366.en. Downloaded on 13 October 2018.

Bond, J., 1945. *Check-List of Birds of The West Indies*. The Academy of Natural Sciences of Philadelphia.

Bond, J., 1950. *Check-List of Birds of The West Indies*. The Academy of Natural Sciences of Philadelphia; Third Edition.

Bond, J., 1948. Origin of the bird fauna of the West Indies. *Wilson Bulletin* 60:207–229.

Bond, J., 1985. *Birds of the West Indies, A Guide to the species of Birds that inhabit the Greater Antilles, Lesser Antilles and Bahama Islands*, fifth Edition. Collins.

Blanco, P., 2006. Distribución y áreas de importancia para las aves del orden Charadriiformes en Cuba. Tesis en opción al grado científico de Doctor en Ciencias Biológicas, Instituto de Ecología y Sistemática, La Habana.

Blanco, P. y B. Sánchez, 2005. Recuperación de Aves Migratorias Neárticas del Orden Anseriformes en Cuba. *Journal of Caribbean Ornithology*. 18:1–6.

Blanco, P. y B. Sánchez, 2011. Nuevas Categorías de Permanencia para Especies del Orden Charadriiformes en Cuba. *Journal of Caribbean Ornithology*. 24:20–25.

Brewer, D., 2018. Cuban Vireo (*Vireo gundlachii*). In: del Hoyo, J., Elliott, A., Sargatal, J., Christie, D.A. & de Juana, E. (eds.). *Handbook of the Birds of the World Alive*. Lynx Edicions, Barcelona. (retrieved from www.hbw.com/node/61247 on 24 September 2018).

Burns, K. J., P. Unitt and N. A. Mason, 2016. A genus-level classification of the family Thraupidae (Class Aves: Order Passeriformes). *Zootaxa4088* (3): 329–354.

Carboneras, C. & Kirwan, G.M., 2018. Black-bellied Whistling-duck (*Dendrocygna autumnalis*). In: del Hoyo, J., Elliott, A., Sargatal, J., Christie, D.A. & de Juana, E. (eds.). *Handbook of the Birds of the World Alive*. Lynx Edicions, Barcelona. (retrieved from www.hbw.com/node/52801 on 28 September 2018).

Carboneras, C., Jutglar, F. & Kirwan, G.M., 2018. Band-rumped Storm-petrel (*Hydrobates castro*). In: del Hoyo, J., Elliott, A., Sargatal, J., Christie, D.A. & de Juana, E. (eds.). *Handbook of the Birds of the World Alive*. Lynx Edicions, Barcelona. (retrieved from https://www.hbw.com/node/52592 on 23 September 2018).

Carmi, O., Witt, C. C., Jaramillo, A., Dumbacher, J.P., 2015. Phylogeography of the Vermilion Flycatcher species complex: multiple speciation events, shifts in migratory behavior, and an apparent extinction of a Galápagos-endemic bird species, *Molecular Phylogenetics and Evolution* (2016), doi: http://dx.doi.org/10.1016/j.ympev.2016.05.029.

Castro Álvarez, R., L. Mugica, M. Acosta, E. García, G. E. Álvarez. 2018 (*in press*). Avifauna de los humedales del IBA Sur de Pinar del Río, Cuba. *Revista Cubana de Ciencias Biológicas*.

Chesser, R. Terry, Kevin J. Burns, C. Cicero, J. L. Dunn, A. W. Kratter, Irby J. Lovette, Pamela C. Rasmussen, J. V. Remsen, Jr., Douglas F. Stotz, Benjamin M. Winger, and Kevin Winker, 2018. Fifty-ninth Supplement to the American Ornithological Society's Check-list of North American Birds, Volume 135, 2018, pp. 798–813 DOI: 10.1642/*The Auk* -18-62.1.

Chesser, R. T., K. J. Burns, C. Cicero, J. L. Dunn, A. W. Kratter, I. J. Lovette, P. C. Rasmussen, J. V. Remsen, Jr., D. F. Stotz, B. M. Winger, and K. Winker, 2017. Fifty-eighth Supplement to the American Ornithological Society's Check-list of North American Birds, Volume 134, 2017, pp. 751–773 DOI: 10.1642/*The Auk*-17-72.1.

Chesser, R. T., K. J. Burns, C. Cicero, J. L. Dunn, A. W. Kratter, I. J. Lovette, P. C. Rasmussen, J. V. Remsen, Jr., D. F. Stotz, B. M. Winger, and K. Winker, 2017. Fifty-ninth Supplement to the American Ornithological Society's Check-list of North American Birds, Volume 135, 2018, pp. 798–813 DOI: 10.1642/*The Auk* -18-62.1.

Chesser, R. T., R. C. Banks, K. J. Burns, C. Cicero, J. L. Dunn, A. W. Kratter, I. J. Lovette, A. G. Navarro-Sigüenza, P. C. Rasmussen, J. V. Remsen, Jr., J. D. Rising, D. F. Stotz, and K. Winker, 2015. Fifty-sixth Supplement to the American Ornithologists' Union Check-list of North American Birds. The Auk Ornithological Advances, AOU, Volume 132, 2015, pp. 748–764 DOI: 10.1642/*The Auk* -15-73.1.

Chesser, R. T., R. C. Banks, K. J. Burns, C. Cicero, J. L. Dunn, A. W. Kratter, I. J. Lovette, A. G. Navarro-Sigüenza, P. C. Rasmussen, J. V. Remsen, Jr., J. D. Rising, D. F. Stotz, and K. Winker, 2016. Fifty-seventh Supplement to the American Ornithologists' Union Check-list of North American Birds. The Auk Ornithological Advances, AOU, Volume 133, 2016, pp. 544–560 DOI: 10.1642/*The Auk* -16-77.1.

Chesser, T., R. C. Banks, F. Keithbarker, C. Cicero, J. L. Dunn, A. W. Kratter, I. J. Lovette, P. Rasmussen, J. V. Remsen, Jr., J. D. Rising, D. F. Stotz, and K. Winker, 2011. Fifty-Second Supplement to The American Ornithologists' Union Check-List of North American Birds. *The Auk* 128(3):600–613, 2011, The American Ornithologists' Union.

Cleere, N. & Kirwan, G. M., 2018. Antillean Nighthawk (*Chordeiles gundlachii*). In: del Hoyo, J., Elliott, A., Sargatal, J., Christie, D.A. & de Juana, E. (eds.). *Handbook of the Birds of the World Alive*. Lynx Edicions, Barcelona. (retrieved from https://www.hbw.com/node/55167 on 28 September 2018).

Clement, P. & Sharpe, C.J., 2018. Red Siskin (*Spinus cucullatus*). In: del Hoyo, J., Elliott, A., Sargatal, J., Christie, D.A. & de Juana, E. (eds.). *Handbook of the Birds of the World Alive*. Lynx Edicions, Barcelona. (retrieved from www.hbw.com/node/61345 on 26 September 2018).

Clement, P. & de Juana, E., 2018. Pine Siskin (*Spinus pinus*). In: del Hoyo, J., Elliott, A., Sargatal, J., Christie, D.A. & de Juana, E. (eds.). *Handbook of the Birds of the World Alive*. Lynx Edicions, Barcelona. (retrieved from www.hbw.com/node/61341 on 3 December 2018).

Collar, N. J., 2011. Taxonomic notes on some Asian babblers (Timaliidae). *Forktail* 27, pp. 100-102.

Collinson, M., D. T. Parkin, A. G. Knox, G. Sangster and A. J. Helbig, 2006. Species limits within the genus *Melanitta*, the scoters. *British Birds* 99, 183–201.

Colorado, J. G., 2013. Validación de la fórmula de Pyle para la identificación del complejo de Atrapamoscas de Traill (*Empidonax* sp., Tyrannidae) empleando análisis discriminante. *Ornitología Neotropical*, 24:359-363.

Craves, J. A. and K. R. Hall, 2003. Notable Bird Sightings from Cuba, Winters 2002 and 2003. *Journal of Caribbean Ornithology*. Vol. 16 No. 1:22-23.

Curson, J. (2018) (b). Northern Waterthrush (*Parkesia noveboracensis*). In: del Hoyo, J., Elliott, A., Sargatal, J., Christie, D.A. & de Juana, E. (eds.). *Handbook of the Birds of the World Alive*. Lynx Edicions, Barcelona. (retrieved from https://www.hbw.com/node/61502 on 24 September 2018).

Curson, J., 2018 (a). Oriente Warbler (*Teretistris fornsi*). In: del Hoyo, J., Elliott, A., Sargatal, J., Christie, D.A. & de Juana, E. (eds.). *Handbook of the Birds of the World Alive*. Lynx Edicions, Barcelona. (retrieved from https://www.hbw.com/node/61519 on 25 September 2018).

Curson, J., 2018. Black-throated Grey Warbler (*Setophaga nigrescens*). In: del Hoyo, J., Elliott, A., Sargatal, J., Christie, D.A. & de Juana, E. (eds.). *Handbook of the Birds of the World Alive*. Lynx Edicions, Barcelona. (retrieved from www.hbw.com/node/61472 on 28 September 2018).

Curson, J., 2018. Olive-capped Warbler (*Setophaga pityophila*). In: del Hoyo, J., Elliott, A., Sargatal, J., Christie, D.A. & de Juana, E. (eds.). *Handbook of the Birds of the World Alive*. Lynx Edicions, Barcelona. (retrieved from https://www.hbw.com/node/61483 on 25 September 2018).

Curson, J., 2018. Yellow-throated Warbler (*Setophaga dominica*). In: del Hoyo, J., Elliott, A., Sargatal, J., Christie, D.A. & de Juana, E. (eds.). *Handbook of the Birds of the World Alive*. Lynx Edicions, Barcelona. (retrieved from https://www.hbw.com/node/61478 on 24 September 2018).

del Hoyo, J., Collar, N. & Kirwan, G.M., 2018. Arctic Herring Gull (*Larus smithsonianus*). In: del Hoyo, J., Elliott, A., Sargatal, J., Christie, D.A. & de Juana, E. (eds.). *Handbook of the Birds of the World Alive*. Lynx Edicions, Barcelona. (retrieved from www.hbw.com/node/467313 on 23 September 2018).

d´Orbigny, A., 1837-1856, Tomo III Mamíferos y Aves. In Sagra, Ramón de la. 1838. *Historia física, política y natural de la isla de Cuba*. Paris: Librería de Arthus Bertrand.

del Hoyo, J., Collar, N. & Kirwan, G.M., 2018. Cory's Shearwater (*Calonectris borealis*). In: del Hoyo, J., Elliott, A., Sargatal, J., Christie, D.A. & de Juana, E. (eds.). *Handbook of the Birds of the World Alive*. Lynx Edicions, Barcelona. (retrieved from www.hbw.com/node/467275 on 23 September 2018).

del Hoyo, J., Collar, N. & Marks, J.S., 2018. Crested Caracara (*Caracara cheriway*). In: del Hoyo, J., Elliott, A., Sargatal, J., Christie, D.A. & de Juana, E. (eds.). *Handbook of the Birds of the World Alive*. Lynx Edicions, Barcelona. (retrieved from www.hbw.com/node/467494 on 25 September 2018).

del Hoyo, J., Collar, N. & Marks, J.S., 2018. Swainson's Thrush (*Catharus swainsoni*). In: del Hoyo, J., Elliott, A., Sargatal, J., Christie, D.A. & de Juana, E. (eds.). *Handbook of the Birds of the World Alive*. Lynx Edicions, Barcelona. (retrieved from www.hbw.com/node/1344017 on 24 September 2018).

del Hoyo, J., Collar, N. & Marks, J.S., 2018. Western Red-legged Thrush (*Turdus rubripes*). In: del Hoyo, J., Elliott, A., Sargatal, J., Christie, D.A. & de Juana, E. (eds.). *Handbook of the Birds of the World Alive*. Lynx Edicions, Barcelona. (retrieved from www.hbw.com/node/1344030 on 24 September 2018).

del Hoyo, J., Collar, N., Kirwan, G.M. & Garcia, E.F.J. (2018). Burmese Collared-dove (*Streptopelia xanthocycla*). In: del Hoyo, J., Elliott, A., Sargatal, J., Christie, D.A. & de Juana, E. (eds.). *Handbook of the Birds of the World Alive*. Lynx Edicions, Barcelona. (retrieved from www.hbw.com/node/467131 on 21 September 2018).

del Hoyo, J., Collar, N., Marks, J.S. & Sharpe, C.J. (2018). Cuban Kite (*Chondrohierax wilsonii*). In: del Hoyo, J., Elliott, A., Sargatal, J., Christie, D.A. & de Juana, E. (eds.). *Handbook of the Birds of the World Alive*. Lynx Edicions, Barcelona. (retrieved from www.hbw.com/node/467343 on 23 September 2018).

Denis, D. y H. M. Salvat Torres, 2006. Análisis de las Recuperaciones de Ejemplares Anillados de Garzas y Cocos (Ciconiiformes) En el Período De 1913 A 1998. *Journal of Caribbean Ornithology*, 19:36-41.

Farnsworth, A. & D. Lebbin, 2018. Cuban Pewee (*Contopus caribaeus*). In: del Hoyo, J., Elliott, A., Sargatal, J., Christie, D.A. & de Juana, E. (eds.). *Handbook of the Birds of the World Alive*. Lynx Edicions, Barcelona. (retrieved from https://www.hbw.com/node/57372 on 22 October 2018).

Fleischer, R. C., J. J. Kirchman, J. P. Dumbacher, L. Bevier, C. Dove, N. C. Rotzel, S. V. Edwards, M. Lammertink, K. J. Miglia and W. S. Moore, 2006. Mid-Pleistocene divergence of Cuban and North American Ivory-billed woodpeckers. *Biology Letters* (2006)2, 466–469 doi:10.1098/rsbl.2006.0490.

Fraga, R., 2018. Red-shouldered Blackbird (*Agelaius assimilis*). In: del Hoyo, J., Elliott, A., Sargatal, J., Christie, D.A. & de Juana, E. (eds.). *Handbook of the Birds of the World Alive*. Lynx Edicions, Barcelona. (retrieved from www.hbw.com/node/62299 on 28 September 2018).

García-Lau, I. y A. González, 2016. Composición de la colección científica de aves del Museo de Historia Natural "Felipe Poey", Universidad de La Habana. *Revista Cubana de Ciencias Biológicas*, Vol.4, Num. 3, 36-42.

Garrido O. H. and F. García, 1975. *Catálogo de las Aves de Cuba*. Edit. Academia de Ciencias de Cuba, La Habana.

Garrido O. H. and J. W. Wiley, 2010. First Cuban Occurrence of Orange Bishop (*Euplectes franciscanus*). *Journal of Caribbean Ornithology*. 23:55–57.

Garrido, O. H. La Gallinuela Norteamericana de Agua Dulce *Rallus elegans elegans* (Aves: Rallidae) en Cuba. *Garciana* No. 10, 1988.

Garrido, O. H., 1995. Preliminary Review on the Short-eared Owl *Asio flammeus* complex in the Greater Antilles. *El Pitirre*, Soc. Carb. Ornithol. Fall 1995. Vol. 8, No. 3. p. 8.

Garrido, O. H., and F. García Montaña. 1967. El "Arrocero Negrito," *Volatinia jacarina splendens* (Vieillot) (Fringillidae: Aves), en Cuba. Trabajo Divulgación, Museo "Felipe Poey," de la Academia de Ciencias de Cuba 50:1–6.

Garrido, O. H., and F. García Montaña. 1968. Nuevos reportes de aves para Cuba. *Torreia*, Nueva Serie No. 4, 13.

Garrido, O. H., and A. Kirkconnell. 2011. *Aves de Cuba*. Comstock P.A. Cornell University Press, Ithaca, NY.

Gerbracht J. and A. Levesque (Unpublished manuscript). . *The Complete Checklist of the Birds of the West Indies*. Checklist Committee, BirdsCaribbean, Arlington, VA.

Gochfeld, M., Burger, J. & Garcia, E.F.J., 2018. Sandwich Tern (*Thalasseus sandvicensis*). In: del Hoyo, J., Elliott, A., Sargatal, J., Christie, D.A. & de Juana, E. (eds.). *Handbook of the Birds of the World Alive*. Lynx Edicions, Barcelona. (retrieved from www.hbw.com/node/54016 on 23 September 2018).

Gochfeld, M., Burger, J., Kirwan, G.M. & Garcia, E.F.J., 2018. Bridled Tern (*Onychoprion anaethetus*). In: del Hoyo, J., Elliott, A., Sargatal, J., Christie, D.A. & de Juana, E. (eds.). *Handbook of the Birds of the World Alive*. Lynx Edicions, Barcelona. (retrieved from www.hbw.com/node/54042 on 23 September 2018).

González A., H., Alejandro Llanes, B. Sánchez, D. Rodríguez, E. Pérez y P. Blanco, 2006. Características de la Migración Otoñal de las Aves Terrestres en Varias Regiones de Cuba. *Journal of Caribbean Ornithology* 19:73-90.

González Alonso, H., L. Rodríguez Schettino, A. Rodríguez, C. A. Mancina e I. Ramos García. 2012. *Libro Rojo de los vertebrados de Cuba*. Editorial Academia, La Habana.

Gundlach, J. C., 1873. Catálogo de las Aves cubanas. *Anales de la Sociedad española de Historia Natural*, Tomo Segundo, Madrid, Don S. de Uhagon, Tesorero, 81-191.

Gundlach, J. C., 1893. *Ornitología cubana*. La Moderna Press, Havana.

Hernández, P. E., 2006. Primer Registro sobre la Reproducción del Ostrero Americano (*Haematopus palliatus*) en Cuba. *Journal of Caribbean Ornithology* 19:59-60.

Herr, Connie Ann, 2011. Phylogeography of a vanishing North American songbird: The Painted Bunting (*Passerina ciris*). UNLV Theses, Dissertations, Professional Papers, and Capstones. 1318.

Holt, D.W., Berkley, R., Deppe, C., Enríquez Rocha, P., Petersen, J.L., R. Salazar, J.L., Segars, K.P., Wood, K.L., Kirwan, G.M. & Marks, J.S., 2018. Bare-legged Screech-owl (*Margarobyas lawrencii*). In: del Hoyo, J., Elliott, A., Sargatal, J., Christie, D.A. & de Juana, E. (eds.). *Handbook of the Birds of the World Alive*. Lynx Edicions, Barcelona. (retrieved from www.hbw.com/node/55002 on 28 September 2018).

Johnson, J. A., R. Thorstrom and D. P. Mindell, 2007. Systematics and conservation of the hook-billed kite including the island taxa from Cuba and Grenada. *Animal Conservation* 10 349–359. The Zoological Society of London.

Kirkconnell A. and Garrido O. H., 1996. La Candelita *Setophaga ruticilla* (Aves: Parulidae) nidificando en Cuba. *El Pitirre*, 9(3): 5.

Kirkconnell A. and Garrido O. H., 1997. El Guincho Americano *Pandion haliaetus carolinensis* (Aves: Pandionidae) anidando en Cuba. *El Pitirre*, 10(2): 64.

Kirkconnell P., A., D. F. Stotz, and J. M. Shopland, eds. 2005. Cuba: *Península de Zapata. Rapid Biological Inventories Report 07*. The Field Museum, Chicago, 150.

Kirkconnell, A. and G. M. Kirwan, 2008. Aves de Cayo Paredón Grande, Archipiélago Sabana-Camagüey, Cuba. *Journal of Caribbean Ornithology* 21:26-36.

Kirwan, G. M., 2001. Further Records of the Northern Potoo (*Nyctibius jamaicensis*) in Cuba, and a Correction to Martínez *et al*. *El Pitirre, Journal of Caribbean Ornithology*. Spring 2001 Vol. 14, No.1.

Labrada, O and P. Blanco, 2011. Permanencia Invernal y Primer Registro de Nidificación de la Avoceta (*Recurvirostra americana*) en Cuba. *Journal of Caribbean Ornithology* 24:71-73.

Llanes Sosa, A., E. Pérez Mena, H. González Alonso, A. Pérez Hernández y P. Rodríguez Casariego, 2016. Nuevos registros de aves para la península de Guanahacabibes, que incluyen el primer registro de *Cardellina pusilla pileolata* para Cuba. *Poeyana*, 502 (enero-junio): 63 - 71, 2016.

Martínez, O., O. H. Garrido, G. B. Reynard, W. Suárez, A. Kirkconnell, and J. W. Wiley, 2000. A New Family and Genus of Birds (Aves: Caprimulgiformes: Nyctibiidae) for Cuba. *El Pitirre*, Society of Caribbean Ornithology. Fall 2000 Vol. 13, No. 3.

Martínez, O., L. Cotayo, A. Kirkconnell & J. W. Wiley, 2016. First record of Lapland Longspur *Calcarius lapponicus* in the *Bulletin of the British Ornithologists' Club*, 136(4).

Martínez-Vilalta, A. Motis & G. M. Kirwan, 2018 (a). Great Blue Heron (*Ardea herodias*). In: del Hoyo, J., Elliott, A., Sargatal, J., Christie, D.A. & de Juana, E. (eds.). *Handbook of the Birds of the World Alive*. Lynx Edicions, Barcelona. (retrieved from www.hbw.com/node/52675 on 23 September 2018).

Martínez-Vilalta, A., Motis, A., D. A. Christie & G. M. Kirwan, 2018 (b). Green-backed Heron (*Butorides striata*). In: del Hoyo, J., Elliott, A., Sargatal, J., Christie, D.A. & de Juana, E. (eds.). *Handbook of the Birds of the World Alive*. Lynx Edicions, Barcelona. (retrieved from https://www.hbw.com/node/52704 on 23 September 2018).

Matheu, E., del Hoyo, J., D. A. Christie, G. M. Kirwan, E. F. J. Garcia & P. Boesman, 2018. White Ibis (*Eudocimus albus and E. ruber*). In: del Hoyo, J., Elliott, A., Sargatal, J., Christie, D.A. & de Juana, E. (eds.). *Handbook of the Birds of the World Alive*. Lynx Edicions, Barcelona. (retrieved from www.hbw.com/node/52773 and 52774 on 28 September 2018).

Matheu, E., J. del Hoyo, G. M. Kirwan, E. F. J. García, & P. Boesman, 2018. Glossy Ibis (*Plegadis falcinellus*). In: del Hoyo, J., Elliott, A., Sargatal, J., Christie, D.A. & de Juana, E. (eds.). *Handbook of the Birds of the World Alive*. Lynx Edicions, Barcelona. (retrieved from www.hbw.com/node/52775 on 23 September 2018).

Mays, H. L. Jr., B. D McKay, D. T. Tietze, Ch. Yao, L. N. Miller, K. Moreland and F. Lei, 2015. A multilocus molecular phylogeny for the avian genus Liocichla (Passeriformes: Leiothrichidae: Liocichla). Mays Jr. *et al*. Avian Research (2015) 6:17 Doi 10.1186/s40657-015-0025-y.

Mears, E. A. 1911. Description of a New Subspecies of the Painted Bunting from the Interior of Texas. *Proceedings of the Biological Society of Washington.*, 24: 217-15.

Navarro, N. and E. Reyes, 2017. *Annotated Checklist of the Birds of Cuba*, Ediciones Nuevos Mundos, St. Augustine, FL, No. 1.

Orta, J., D. A. Christie, E. F. J. Garcia, & P. Boesman, 2018. Magnificent Frigatebird (*Fregata magnificens*). In: del Hoyo, J., Elliott, A., Sargatal, J., Christie, D.A. & de Juana, E. (eds.). *Handbook of the Birds of the World Alive*. Lynx Edicions, Barcelona. (retrieved from https://www.hbw.com/node/52669 on 23 September 2018).

Oswald, J. A.; M. G. Harvey, R. C. Remsen, D. U. Foxworth, S. W. Cardiff, D. L. Dittmann, L. C. Megna, M. D. Carling and R. T. Brumfield, 2016. Willet be one species or two? A genomic view of the evolutionary history of *Tringa semipalmata*. *The Auk Ornithological Advances*, AOU, Volume 133, 2016, pp. 593–614 DOI: 10.1642/AUK-15-232.1.

Payne, R. & G. M. Kirwan, (2018). Cuban Lizard-cuckoo (*Coccyzus merlini*). In: del Hoyo, J., Elliott, A., Sargatal, J., Christie, D.A. & de Juana, E. (eds.). *Handbook of the Birds of the World Alive*. Lynx Edicions, Barcelona. (retrieved from www.hbw.com/node/54897 on 21 September 2018).

Payne, R., 2018. Tricoloured Munia (*Lonchura malacca*). In: del Hoyo, J., Elliott, A., Sargatal, J., Christie, D.A. & de Juana, E. (eds.). *Handbook of the Birds of the World Alive*. Lynx Edicions, Barcelona. (retrieved from www.hbw.com/node/61194 on 24 September 2018).

Pérez, E., P. Rodríguez, D. Rodríguez, A. Parada, O. Barrios, y E. Ruiz, 2005. Primer Registro de *Sterna sandvicensis eurygnatha* para Cuba. *Journal of Caribbean Ornithology*. 18:29-30.

Phillips, A. R., 1948. Geographic variation in *Empidonax traillii*. *The Auk*, Oct. 65: 507-514.

Pyle, P. 1997. *Identification guide to North American birds.* Part I, Columbidae to Ploceidae. Slate Creek Press, Bolinas, CA.

Raffaele, H., J. Wiley, O. Garrido, A. Keith, and J. Raffaele. 1998. *A Guide to the Birds of the West Indies*. Princeton University Press, Princeton, NJ.

Ragues, P. V., 1914. *Museo cubano "Gundlach", Catálogo general*. Instituto de Segunda Enseñanza de la Habana. Imprenta Cuba Intelectual, Habana, Santo Tomás 30, Cerro.

Regalado, P., 1975. Primer Hallazgo de *Speotyto cunicularia* (Molina) anidando en Cuba. *Revista Forestal Baracoa, Cuba;* Publicación Científico Técnica Año 5 No. 1-2, 36-56.

Ridgway, R. 1894. *Colinus virginianus cubanensis* is not a Florida bird. *The Auk* 11:324–325.

Rising, J. & D. A. Christie, 2018. Lapland Longspur (*Calcarius lapponicus*). In: del Hoyo, J., Elliott, A., Sargatal, J., Christie, D.A. & de Juana, E. (eds.). *Handbook of the Birds of the World Alive*. Lynx Edicions, Barcelona. (retrieved from www.hbw.com/node/61854 on 24 September 2018).

Rising, J., 2018. Black-faced Grassquit (*Melanospiza bicolor*). In: del Hoyo, J., Elliott, A., Sargatal, J., Christie, D.A. & de Juana, E. (eds.). *Handbook of the Birds of the World Alive*. Lynx Edicions, Barcelona. (retrieved from https://www.hbw.com/node/62154 on 25 September 2018).

Rising, J., 2018. Cuban Grassquit (*Phonipara canora*). In: del Hoyo, J., Elliott, A., Sargatal, J., Christie, D.A. & de Juana, E. (eds.). *Handbook of the Birds of the World Alive*. Lynx Edicions, Barcelona. (retrieved from https://www.hbw.com/node/62151 on 25 September 2018.

Rodríguez Casariego, P., A. Parada Isada, E. Pérez Mena, D. Rodríguez Batista, O. Barrios, E. Ruiz Rojas, y P. Blanco Rodríguez, 2008. Primer Registro de Nidificación del Pampero de Audubon (*Puffinus Lherminieri*) en Cuba. *Journal of Caribbean Ornithology*. 21:44-45.

Rodríguez Batista, D., E. Ruiz Rojas, A. Parada Isada y A. Hernández Muños, 2014. Composición y distribución de las Aves pp. 218-338. En Rodríguez Batista, D., A. Arias Barreto y E. Ruiz Rojas (eds). 2014. *Fauna terrestre del Archipielago de Sabana-Camagüey, Cuba*. Editorial Academia, La Habana.

Rodríguez Castaneda, Y. and J. W. Wiley, 2015. Probable first breeding record of Indigo Bunting (Passerina cyanea; family Cardinalidae) in the West Indies. *The Journal of Caribbean Ornithology*, Vol. 28:22–24.

Rodríguez Castaneda, Y., J. W. Wiley, and O. H. Garrido, 2017. Additional records of Lazuli Bunting (*Passerina amoena*) and first records of several wild-caught exotic birds for Cuba. *The Journal of Caribbean Ornithology*, Vol. 30(2):134–142.

Sangster, G., 2008. A revision of *Vermivora* (Parulidae), with the description of a new genus. *Bulletin of the British Ornithologists' Club*, 128(3).

Schuchmann, K. L., G. M. Kirwan, & de Juana, E., 2018. Bahama Woodstar (*Calliphlox evelynae*). In: del Hoyo, J., Elliott, A., Sargatal, J., Christie, D.A. & de Juana, E. (eds.). *Handbook of the Birds of the World Alive*. Lynx Edicions, Barcelona. (retrieved from www.hbw.com/node/55645 on 28 September 2018).

Seutin, G., 1991. Morphometric Identification of Traill´s Flycatchers: An Assessment of Stein´s Formula. *Journal of Field Ornithologist*, 62(3):308-313.

Thompson, Ch. W., 1991. Is The Painted Bunting Actually Two Species? Problems Determining Species Limits Between Allopatric Populations. *The Condor* 93:987-1000.

Tweit, R. C., 2014. Split *Passerina pallidior* from Painted Bunting *P. ciris*. *In* AOU Classification Committee-North and Middle America, Proposal Set 2015-A-7, pp. 638-639.

Van Gils, J., P. Wiersma & P. Boesman, 2018. Sanderling (*Calidris alba*). In: del Hoyo, J., Elliott, A., Sargatal, J., Christie, D.A. & de Juana, E. (eds.). *Handbook of the Birds of the World Alive*. Lynx Edicions, Barcelona. (retrieved from www.hbw.com/node/53923 on 28 September 2018).

Van Gils, J., Wiersma, P. & Kirwan, G. M., 2018. Whimbrel (*Numenius phaeopus*). In: del Hoyo, J., Elliott, A., Sargatal, J., Christie, D.A. & de Juana, E. (eds.). *Handbook of the Birds of the World Alive*. Lynx Edicions, Barcelona. (retrieved from www.hbw.com/node/53894 on 22 September 2018).

Van Gils, J., P. Wiersma, & G. M. Kirwan, 2018. Wilson's Phalarope (*Steganopus tricolor*). In: del Hoyo, J., Elliott, A., Sargatal, J., Christie, D.A. & de Juana, E. (eds.). *Handbook of the Birds of the World Alive*. Lynx Edicions, Barcelona. (retrieved from www.hbw.com/node/53944 on 23 September 2018).

Watson G. E., 1962. Notes on the Spotted Rail in Cuba. *The Wilson Bulletin*, December 1962 Vol. 74, No. 4.

Williford, D. L'Amour, 2013. Molecular Genetics of the Northern Bobwhite, Scaled Quail, and Gambel's

Quail. Dissertation, submitted to the office of graduate studies of Texas A&M University–Kingsville; in partial fulfillment of the requirements for the degree of Doctor of Philosophy.

Winkler, H. & D. A. Christie, 2018. West Indian Woodpecker (*Melanerpes superciliaris*). In: del Hoyo, J., Elliott, A., Sargatal, J., Christie, D.A. & de Juana, E. (eds.). *Handbook of the Birds of the World Alive*. Lynx Edicions, Barcelona. (retrieved from www.hbw.com/node/56173 on 23 September 2018).

Winkler, H., D. A. Christie, & G. M. Kirwan, 2018. Cuban Green Woodpecker (*Xiphidiopicus percussus*). In: del Hoyo, J., Elliott, A., Sargatal, J., Christie, D.A. & de Juana, E. (eds.). *Handbook of the Birds of the World Alive*. Lynx Edicions, Barcelona. (retrieved from www.hbw.com/node/56180 on 23 September 2018).

Winkler, H., D. A. Christie, & G. M. Kirwan, 2018. Yellow-shafted Flicker (*Colaptes auratus*). In: del Hoyo, J., Elliott, A., Sargatal, J., Christie, D.A. & de Juana, E. (eds.). *Handbook of the Birds of the World Alive*. Lynx Edicions, Barcelona. (retrieved from www.hbw.com/node/56268 on 23 September 2018).

Wunderle, J. M., R. Waide, B. Sánchez y D. Rodríguez. 1992. Primera observación de *Vermivora virginiae* (Aves: Emberizidae) en Cuba. *Comunicaciones breves de Zoología*, Instituto de Ecología y Sistemática, Academia de Ciencias de Cuba: 4.

Yntena, L. D., D. B. McNair, C. Cramer-Burke, F. W. Sladen, J. M. Valiulis, C. D. Lombard, A. O. Lance, and Sh. L. Fromer, 2017. Records and observations of breeding waterbirds, rare and uncommon birds, and marked individuals on St. Croix, U.S. Virgin Islands. *Journal of Caribbean ornithology*, Vol.30 (2):88-127.

Notes

Notes

Printed in Great Britain
by Amazon